THE TROUBLE WITH NATIONAL ACTION

by Mark Hayes

First edition, printed 2019
ISBN 978-1-904491-34-7

Published by
Freedom Press
84b Whitechapel High St,
London
E1 7QX
freedompress.org.uk

CONTENTS

RECOMMENDATIONS

Anyone concerned about the re-emergence of fascism in Britain should read this account of National Action because the analysis it provides is undoubtedly correct. Sometimes direct action is necessary to confront Nazi groups and it is better that local communities deal with the problem rather than relying on the State.

~ Pat Muldowney
ex-member, AFA

This text constitutes an important intervention, offering significant insights into a subterranean world. The continual analysis of Britain's far right is essential to our understanding of its ongoing presence in society.

~ Prof Matthew Worley
University of Reading

In this timely account of National Action Mark Hayes presents a succinct, comprehensively researched and fearless analysis. It is essential reading for all those concerned to understand and address the threat of fascism in modern Britain. Hayes reminds us that while direct action has had success in preventing the growth of some groups, the ideology itself continues to fester within the capitalist system.

~ Dr Paul Aylward
Flinders University

This short book offers a rich and important examination of the very real dangers presented by an apparently new form of Nazism in the UK.

~ Dr Peter Wilkin
Brunel University

At a time when the far right appears to be on the march again this text provides a timely contribution to our knowledge of the phenomenon. Using an in-depth and incisive analysis of one particular form of fascist organisation Hayes argues that while the far right needs to be directly confronted, it cannot be viewed in isolation from the wider global capitalist economic order which contributes to its growth. This important text should be read by all in academia interested in understanding the growth of fascism, and all who are concerned with reversing it.

~ Dr Feilim O'hAdmaill
University College Cork

Carefully researched and elegantly written, Mark Hayes' analysis of National Action is a meticulous account of the practical and ideological connections that link modern, organised fascism directly to the authoritarian capitalist state. His conclusions point to the established structural networks that have cultivated NA, along with the political interests that it so violently serves. This study provides indispensable reading for anti-fascists everywhere.

~ Dr Deaglan O'Donghaile
Liverpool John Moores University

Preface

This short text examines the emergence of a relatively new (and short-lived) Nazi organisation in Britain — National Action. A considered analysis of primary source materials (which are no longer publicly available) reveals that National Action (NA) articulated a particularly uncompromising version of Nazi ideology. The text considers the ideology, strategy and tactics deployed by the group, which engaged in high profile activities that captured the attention of the mainstream and social media. It is noted that NA had a distinct propensity for violence which led not only to street confrontation, but to the expression of certain paramilitary pretensions. The emergence of organisations like National Action is indicative of the on-going threat posed by political elements who refuse to relinquish their adherence to the Nazi creed. Such was the impact made by National Action it led to the organisation being proscribed under the terms of anti-terrorist legislation in Britain.

The aim of this brief analysis is to use the example of National Action to illustrate more precisely the nature of Nazi ideology as a schema based upon a toxic combination of xenophobic nationalism, racism (cultural/genetic), anti-Semitism, a belief in the utility of dictatorship and a commitment to an overtly authoritarian state. The objective is to highlight the persistence of the threat posed by such groups, by stressing the importance of exogenous factors in their continued survival. Observations are thereby made about the reasons for the stubborn persistence of the Nazi creed in Britain and beyond. Such organisations should not be summarily dismissed as irrelevant, obscurantist political cults because even the most miniscule neo-Nazi cliques possess the capacity to do damage to the social fabric and may, in certain circumstances, influence the issue/policy agenda. Moreover, this analysis concludes that the examination of marginal, esoteric political groups should be related more explicitly to the dominant ideology of neoliberalism and an emerging State authoritarianism which provides the socio-economic and political context within which such groups have emerged and continue to exist. The era of austerity, the "war on terror" and Brexit have dramatically altered the overall political inflection in Parliament and beyond, and populist impulses are shifting the ideological centre of gravity toward the far right, making it far easier for fascist ideas to gain traction. This contribution to the debate aims to draw attention to the dangers inherent in this process and the inadequacy of an over-reliance on the State as the primary responder to the menace of fascism. There are clear lessons to be drawn here for anti-fascist activists in Britain and elsewhere.

This text is dedicated to militant anti-fascists everywhere and I would like to thank Freedom Press for allowing me the opportunity to articulate my thoughts (some of which have been developed elsewhere).

Supporting radical publishers is an obligation for all activists on the left and I am happy to donate any revenue accrued from this publication to Freedom Press. I should also like to dedicate this short work to two particular anti-fascists: firstly, to my friend and comrade Eddie O'Neill who, as a Republican volunteer served many years in British prisons, and now plays a crucial role in FIBI (Friends of the International Brigades Ireland); secondly, to Allison Burns, anam cara.

In solidarity,

~ Mark Hayes
Southampton September 2019

The trouble
with National Action

There is no doubt that the apparent escalation of racist incidents, as a consequence of Brexit, has thrown the nature of right-wing "extremist" organisations into a much sharper light. Many of these political factions, which inhabit the fringes of the far right, have very little interest in contesting elections or engaging in conventional constitutional processes — their aim is simply to sustain and promote a specific version of fascist ideology.

The fact that several such groups are now being monitored by State security agencies as potential "terrorist" entities indicates the seriousness with which the British authorities are taking the threat they pose. Senior security figures, such as the head of MI5 Andrew Parker and Neil Basu, who coordinates counter-terrorist policing strategy, have warned of the "serious threat" from rapidly growing right-wing sects. According to one account, Prevent referrals for individuals holding such "extreme" views has increased 36% in the last year alone[1]. Far right groups, advocating violence in pursuit of white supremacist ideals, are obviously back on the agenda, and the British State is beginning to focus on the possible consequences of such political activism.

One such organisation, National Action (NA) which actually referred to itself as a "terror machine" was proscribed in December 2016 under the terms of Britain's anti-terrorism legislation by the Home Secretary Amber Rudd[2]. It is now a criminal offence to be a member of National Action, participate in its meetings or support the organisation in any way. National Action is the first far right organisation to be banned in Britain under the terms of the current anti-terror legislation and anyone found contravening the law could face up to ten years in prison[3]. Judicial intervention effectively ended the organisation in its chosen form, and NA became part of the same MI5 anti-terrorist portfolio which is designed to deal with Islamic jihadis and the plethora of paramilitary organisations which still exist in Northern Ireland. National Action was therefore proscribed as a major threat to national security in Britain.

In fact National Action enthusiastically embraced the epithet "Nazi", indeed the organisation claimed to be at the forefront of a "new wave" of fascist activism in Britain. It is interesting to note that NA represented an explicit rejection of the recent populist trend which had become identifiable in fascist politics across Europe in recent years. This populist attempt to achieve political success by toning down the fascist message, while complying with constitutional methods and adopting a radical right-wing agenda, has been the predominant modus operandi of fascist parties and movements in the contemporary era. In Britain, for example, the British National Party (BNP) expended some considerable energy trying to become "respectable" and electorally viable whilst attempting to conceal its inner ideology, which was nevertheless still identifiably fascist[4]. In this sense the fascists leading the BNP were deliberately trying to camouflage their ideological perspective with a more populist discourse which focused on the issue of preserving British culture and identity. Hence the term "populism", in the context of right-wing political activity, has undoubtedly facilitated the legitimation of certain parties and policies with discernible fascist features. However, the "new wave", as reflected in the ideology and practice of National Action, represented a distinct dismissal of this (ostensibly) more "moderate" approach. Of course the BNP, despite making an initial electoral impact at a local level, was unable to sustain its success, and the far right in Britain today is totally divided, consisting of a variety of much smaller disparate elements. In fact Jackson makes the general observation that "since the fall of the Nazi regime, and the discrediting of fascism as a viable ideology in the eyes of the political mainstream across the world, the myriad post-war reinventions of Nazism, and other variants of fascism, have become far more limited in their political ambitions in the short-term"[5]. This is a particularly pertinent comment in the British context, given the collapse of the BNP's electoral pretensions after 2010 and the apparent demise of the populist variant of fascist praxis. The way was opened up for an alternative agenda and National Action had no apparent interest in conventional politics or developing a more electorally credible populist agenda, but constituted a straightforward, single-minded determination to return to the rigorous first principles of a hard-line Nazi perspective.

National Action, as one of the more recent manifestations of fascism in Britain, certainly attracted some sustained attention from the media, which became fascinated by its unapologetic and uncompromising defence of Nazi ideology. Naturally there is a tendency in the media to exaggerate their coverage of "extremism" for its own purposes, however, the dangers of generating a "moral panic" notwithstanding, the media did nevertheless identify some of the more extraordinary elements which characterised NA. As Cortbus remarked: "what is new and threatening about National Action as a phenomenon is the group's overt, totally unconcealed admiration for Adolf Hitler, its links to the ideology of violent terrorists, and most significantly the advanced, potentially ground-breaking propaganda tactics the group employs"[6]. Indeed, it might be argued that in some ways National Action represented a brand new style of fascist activism in Britain and at one point, as Matthew Collins (an ex-member of the National Front, now writing for *HOPE not Hate* magazine) claimed, NA was in the process of "taking the far right by storm"[7].

Origins, organisation, strategy and tactics

National Action was formed in 2013 as a semi-clandestine group advocating the neo-Nazi ideology of "revolutionary nationalism". Actually NA members saw themselves as the faithful soldiers of the original National Socialist credo, "the living instrument of a well-founded belief" whose aim was to "maintain the independence and agency of our idea"[8]. The emphasis within NA was on practical activism and ideological purity in order to produce what one of its leading members referred to as "an exciting new interpretation of nationalism"[9]. According to Collins, "the new organisation prided itself on being secure, confident, brash and outrageous"[10]. However, it is important to note that NA considered itself to be an association rather than an ordinary political entity (such as a party) maintaining, therefore, that it did not require any formal internal hierarchy: "Instead of a 'leader' we have personalities, instead of officers we have collective talent"[11]. Nevertheless it would be accurate to say that Benjamin Raymond (Benjamin Noyles, former member of the Integralist Party and New British Union), Alex Davies (a former member of the BNP's youth wing) and (latterly) Christopher Lythgoe became the most identifiable leaders of the new group, which held its first conference in 2015. The unambiguous aim of the organisation was to return to a particular conception of national socialist ideology, as articulated originally by Adolf Hitler and the NSDAP (Nationalsozialistische Deutsche Arbeiterpartei), whilst vociferously rejecting more conventional efforts at political activity, particularly elections. Electoral politics, according to NA, inevitably resulted in the dilution of long cherished political ideals. The objective was, in short, to precipitate a paradigmatic shift in neo-Nazi political values on the far right and in the process produce "a cohesive nationalist youth culture"[12].

The origins of National Action lay in the spectacular collapse of the British National Party (BNP) which imploded after its electoral ambitions were forestalled in 2010. The dramatic demise of the BNP, which once held over 50 local council seats, one seat in the London Assembly and had two members in the European Parliament, effectively released a relatively large number of right-wing activists into the ideological ether, with some seeking a return to a more robust articulation of Nazi aspirations. The immediate forerunner of National Action, it could be argued, was English National Resistance, led by former BNP activists Kieran Trent and Matthew Tait, but its origins might also be found in other micro-groups like Islands of the North Atlantic (IONA), the Traditional Britain Group and the Integralist Party. Internet discussion groups like "Western Springs" were also significant in providing a forum where far right activists could gather to exchange ideas and examine how unreconstructed fascists might re-group and recalibrate their political praxis. National Action was one practical outcome of this process of critical self-examination on the fringes of fascist politics in Britain. Significantly, at the outset, the "drunken yobs" that appeared to coalesce around the "centrist" English Defence League (EDL) were rejected by NA as a "charade", and it also unambiguously dismissed the failed electoral strategy of the BNP as a "vanity project"[13]. National Action set itself the task of distancing itself from both single-issue protest politics and conventional (populist) constitutional methods.

In essence, National Action had a very particular political purpose, as the NA website proclaimed: "National Action is a National Socialist youth organisation which means our clientele are clean, intelligent, and ambitious people typically in their late teens or twenties. It is a scene for young Nationalists to network, engage socially, and be creative at a time when there is no prospect for a political success"[14]. As the NA "Strategy and Promotion" document explained: "We have been presented with an opportunity for this project as our market exploits a doldrum period in nationalism where there is no clear nationalist party to get behind"[15]. The overall objective was put, quite succinctly, by NA: "Our whole strategy places value on the public expression of a hard line and determined ideology"[16]. The timing, NA argued, was right to return to primary principles. Moreover nationalists, according to NA, should never compromise on their convictions because "the arrival of fascism in the 20th century was the greatest event in world history … It is not an empty task we now undertake in reviving it"[17].

The organisation itself was only numbered in the hundreds, but it was growing very rapidly and consisted of committed neo-Nazi activists from across Britain, although the biggest area of strength was considered to be the North West[18]. National Action activists also saw themselves as an organisation of elite "stormtroopers", which was emphatically "not for plebs"[19]. The emphasis was also on attracting younger recruits, and there was an informal age limit of 35[20].

Whilst acknowledging the sense of ideological purpose which provided NA's fundamental underlying dynamic (which will be evaluated later), it is important to examine in greater detail the nature of the organisation.

The significance of youth culture:
Style and provocation

This focus on youth was self-evidently designed to facilitate a vibrant and creative cultural milieu, as NA documentation put it: "Youth is more than just a demographic — it is the basis of having a 'scene'"[21]. The group stressed the need to attract young nationalist "heroes" who possessed the vision, not only to construct a network of cadres, but to "build a war machine that can tear through the tired institutions and rip them into bloody shreds"[22]. Indeed, National Action often criticised "other forms of British extreme right politics for failing to develop an exciting aesthetic style that attracts a new generation to openly fascist politics … So National Action has attempted to turn its extreme politics into a new 'look', to distinguish it from other components in the British neo-Nazi milieu"[23].

With this in mind, NA was designed to purvey neo-Nazi nationalism, not just as a set of ideas, but as a "way of life" and a lived experience. National Action therefore aimed to provide a secure space for neo-Nazi activists to exchange ideas and interact, in order to generate a vigorous and effective neo-fascist network. Interestingly, those leading NA were well aware of the significance of contemporary fashion to young people: "Part of raising the social status of nationalism is going to be providing a look — a style that is fashionable … ideally this has to be for an urban environment. Developing this look has always been a balancing act between awkward overdressing, and pub slobs" but the aim was "to somehow become chic"[24]. National Action, dressed predominantly in the clothing brand White Rex (linked to Russian white supremacist martial arts), aimed to make fascism de rigueur. It has been argued that, in recent years, the "fascist fashion" milieu has moved gradually away from the more obvious skinhead style, and more towards the "bland" and "benign" in an effort to "camouflage itself within mainstream society"[25]. Although this may be true for the populist far right in a more generalised sense, NA's attempt to construct a highly visual, aesthetic sub-cultural differentiation was in some ways a clear rejection of this particular trend.

In order to convey its message NA utilised the most evocative imagery, whilst professionally produced graphics were designed to create an immediate emotional impact which was focused primarily on alienated white youth in Britain. The NA website, which launched in September 2013, aimed to attract attention and antagonise political adversaries. Lurid images and provocative language featured prominently ("we are going to gas sub-human communist scum") which was combined with heavily edited footage of their practical activities. Interventions on the website were invariably confrontational, racist and virulently anti-Semitic (see later). Self-evidently NA traded in extravagant, theatrical bravado on the blogosphere, whilst attempting to offer easy access to excitement and adventure via participation in their so-called "white jihad". Internet forums and the dark web were also used explicitly to attract potential recruits and NA had Facebook, Tumblr and Twitter accounts providing a more open space which enabled both carefully planned and more unpredictable forms of communicative interaction. Podcasts such as *The Voice of Albion* were also used to promote ideas. The internet thus provided the intimacy required to act as an echo chamber to cultivate support and facilitated the capacity to induce opposition which was designed to re-enforce the process of political radicalisation. The internet provided both an uncensored mechanism to "correct the lies" of the mainstream media and a forum which was suitable for the expression of solidarity and the mobilisation of support. For NA the new technology offered a positive pathway toward greater visibility and accessibility by purveying its political message across the entire range of the new-media eco-system. Moreover, according to NA, it alone possessed the courage to pioneer such an aggressive form of agitprop which was "irreverent", "extreme", and designed for "shock value" because "hardcore propaganda" suited its purpose as an organisation[26]. For example, after the far right activist Thomas Mair had murdered Labour MP Jo Cox (whilst shouting "death to traitors, freedom for Britain"), NA posted the statement "only 649 to go". Hence it has been noted that NA became, in a very short time frame, "masters of marketing, often seizing on tragedy to super-charge the repugnance of their rhetoric", and as NA itself confirmed: "Whether we are pitching this idea to other nationalists or to the public we need our words to come in hammer blows"[27].

The objective of National Action was to build, via bellicose and belligerent propaganda, an organisation that was resilient and determined, and able to command respect. To achieve this NA required people who possessed not only ideological commitment but, crucially, the capacity to fight. National Action stressed the need for participants who were much more committed to the cause than mere followers. The members had to be the "fighting element" which would "remain pure" in their adherence to their political religion[28]. The sense of conveying a messianic mission was clearly evident: "Only a movement of strength lives in appreciation for the task of survival and the victory that will come. Only when you establish a power relationship with your enemies do you exist in a state of struggle and have any bargaining power"[29]. As Raymond put it: "One day there will be a time for civilised discussion maybe, but we can't do that until we make them respect us — now they are going to get their heads kicked in"[30]. This explicit emphasis on violence was evident in much of NA's output, although NA claimed to act within the law, indeed, NA at times claimed to be an advocacy group which suggested a certain familiarity with the law on conspiracy in this regard[31]. Assertions by NA about its law-abiding intent are, however, difficult to sustain given the extremely aggressive rhetoric utilised and the provocative tactics persistently deployed by the group. Clearly the claims made about legality constituted a straightforward tactical manoeuvre in an effort to avoid unwanted attention from the police. Ultimately, of course, this evasion failed.

Certainly some of NA's activities were designed, at the very least, to provoke a response, for example distributing unambiguous pro-Nazi leaflets in major multicultural cities like Birmingham, Coventry and Liverpool. NA held their first "white man" march in Newcastle in 2015 and aimed to repeat the activity elsewhere. Indeed, in Liverpool in 2015 NA threatened to start a race riot, claiming boastfully that "only bullets will stop us"[32]. Although, on the day NA activists were forced into an ignominious retreat, the NA website maintained that "by leafleting in the heart of a cosmopolitan metropolis, we have shown that no matter how radical the message or how multiracial the area, Nationalists have no reason to fear going out on the streets and spreading the message"[33].

National Action also organised "flash-mobs" on University campuses (e.g. Warwick University), and NA claimed to have a presence in some British Universities[34]. This type of semi-spontaneous "propaganda of the deed" afforded NA a significant tactical advantage because it effectively deprived the anti-fascist opposition of the opportunity to mobilise[35]. Furthermore, the fact that NA was unconcerned about the reaction it received, as a consequence of its activities, was most vividly illustrated when its members posted pictures of themselves on the internet giving Nazi salutes in the so-called "corpse cellar" at Buchenwald concentration camp in May 2016[36]. The media outrage at such an act was entirely predictable. The mainstream media was used therefore, not in an attempt to seek approval or solicit wider support, but to instil fear and raise their political profile by shocking the sensibilities of the general public.

Obviously the emphasis in NA was on boots not suits with a consistent, if controversial, message and a relatively high level of organisational competence. There is also evidence that, if left to their own devices, their tactics may well have moved beyond the puerile macho posturing of street confrontation. In 2014 NA members took part in a "Sigurd Outlaw Camp" in the Brecon Beacons which suggested a mindset that was looking toward the deployment of more paramilitary methods. For instance, there was some discussion, in NA circles, of the "one-man cell" as a "functioning instrument" which reflected a need to convey the impression that NA was "a group of action not just words" intent on making a tangible impact on the political landscape[37]. This was expressed clearly on the NA website: "To achieve our objectives we must at first use tactics such as those established by Louis Beam's model of Leaderless Resistance which encourages the adoption of a phantom cell structure rather than a tiered and hierarchical form of army. Beam's strategy needs to inform our initial engagements with the hegemonic forces who seek to suppress us"[38].

Hence "lone wolf" attacks, which are notoriously difficult to prevent because the activist operates independently of leaders or movement, were explicitly encouraged in NA's online literature. In short, in the absence of popular support, the NA Nazi activist was encouraged to resort to the "despairing bravado" of the autonomous assassin in an effort to precipitate chaos and make a political point[39]. As NA explained: "We want things to get worse so that the system burns its bridges ... worse is better'[40]. Clearly, as Matthew Collins pointed out, the organisation was "hell-bent on continuing its provocative actions" and the individuals within NA were "becoming increasingly erratic, unpredictable and potentially violent"[41].

Ideology: the neo-Nazi weltanschauung

If we look more specifically at the political ideas and concepts articulated by National Action we can see that it sought to position itself with reference to the ideological heritage of fascism — all the familiar Nazi ideological themes were evident in the NA credo. These ideas will now be outlined and examined in more detail.

Firstly, NA evidently expressed a desire for action and romantic adventure which clearly underpins various types of fascism. In fascist ideology the need for immediate action always transcends the sterile emphasis on sedentary reflection. As NA put it, "no loss as a consequence of acting can be greater than the loss from failing to act. There is no acceptable excuse for not acting. If we do not act then everything will be lost"[42]. Indeed NA argued that "in political struggle the most sacred and important task is to find the Holy Grail of Action"[43]. Moreover, in essence, fascism constitutes a fundamental appeal to emotions and instincts, as NA put it: "The mind follows the heart", "man is not a rational being but a rationalising one — strength of imagery and deeds will win hearts and minds"[44]. Fascist vitalism therefore insists that faith precedes, and takes precedence over, reason.

In fact, according to NA, "the more stylish, decadent and ferocious European nationalism appears, the more irresistible it will become in the eyes of young Europeans. An entire generation will be intoxicated by danger, duty, discipline and destiny"[45]. As NA activist Raymond pointed out, "fascism has a romantic allure that is quite visibly missing from modern politics"[46]. National Action claimed that "hard line fascism and National Socialism are the generic default for (young) people because that is the point along the political spectrum at which resistance starts. It is a point that transcends politics because it is understood not through argument but through emotion which is universal and accessible"[47]. The implication is quite evident: "People are never won by the rights and wrongs of factions and arguments, the people are only ever won by emotion"[48]. According to the fascist perspective, as articulated by NA, the over-emphasis on theory simply erodes healthy instincts: "You don't have to be smart to get the truth; it is something that is felt"[49]. Hence NA unambiguously stressed the need to return to pre-rational instincts: "The best among us are not the intelligent, but those with good instincts. The truly committed are those who fight from the heart" and "the Fascist experiment has proven that the vital Instinct of a people can be cultivated to the creation of idealistic fanatics"[50]. NA were perfectly prepared to reiterate the point: "We do not need 'intellectuals', what we need are brutes ... who can rise above fear ... only a storm of flowing passion will save our people"[51].

The belief that life was a perpetual struggle was also a characteristic of fascism, an ideology which was permeated by distorted social Darwinist preconceptions about human existence. According to NA "the truth is that life is struggle and those who refuse to engage in the struggle for life perish" therefore "we need something that is vitalistic and visceral — that drives us to be different to everything that flourishes in our sick world … a world where the law of the jungle demand vicious animals to fight for survival"[52]. As a consequence, NA maintained that "spirit must prevail over matter" and "a dozen determined men can overcome a disorganised rabble of 100" therefore NA argued that "we must seek to make ourselves a conductor, a lightning rod which concentrates and amplifies the vague menacing tension and rage that is slowly mounting across British society"[53]. The struggle would be long and difficult but once the strongest had prevailed the rewards would be worth it, as NA put it: "There will be rebuilding, it will be a complete nightmare … but one day — it will all be ours. It will be beautiful beyond our wildest dreams"[54]. The "new order" would emerge from the competitive chaos that fascism identified as an inescapable component of human existence. Moreover, the contemporary socio-economic and political situation was seen as ripe for a new generation of Nazi nationalists to lead a new, apocalyptic struggle for survival.

Of course, nationalism was a central element in the ideological discourse of fascism. For the original fascists the nation was the focus of extreme loyalty which fosters a sense of collective identity, and the interests of the nation-state should transcend individual self-interest and class sectionalism. Classical fascists were fanatical exponents of ultra-nationalism. So too National Action: "We are nationalists fighting for the people"[55]. However, as far as NA was concerned, this nationalism needed to be a "new" version, not populist, "respectable", or the "plastic patriotism" which panders to what is acceptable to the general population[56]. As NA argued: "The type of patriotism we promote has to be relevant" since "the Empire is dead and the kind of flag-waving that worked for our grandfathers' generation, appeals to a patriotic duty that just doesn't exist anymore" so "our concept of Britain is a promise of what is to come"[57]. The Nazis in NA stressed the need for renewal, national palingenesis and a new Britain.

Nationalism, from the NA perspective, also needed to be seen as a desirable lifestyle choice rather than an anachronistic chore, so it had to be "fashionable, good looking, cool" and "confident", facilitated by a like-minded social network[58]. As NA said, "maintaining the purity of nationalism so that it doesn't run off the tracks is like dog breeding or any other racial science" which requires "eliminating runts"[59]. National Action claimed that British nationalism was an unhealthy creature because it had persistently tolerated treason, therefore a pristine "New Order" was required where a more assertive and aggressive nationalism would sit at the apex of the social value framework. At which point, "gone will be the self-hate and sickly pacifism that nearly destroyed us. Heroism, Courage, Self-Sacrifice, too long condemned as militaristic tendencies of which we should be ashamed, shall be recognised once more as the greatest attributes of the British race"[60]. Thus nationalism, assertive, jingoistic and xenophobic, was situated at the epicentre of National Action's view of the world.

Naturally, in the new nationalist dispensation advocated by NA, there would be no place for democratic structures. As NA put it: "The people are lost, having been 'given' democracy, they do not know what to do with it and are easily beguiled and seduced by cunning propaganda", "the people have had their go at self-government and blown it"[61]. Indeed, "those that gain influence or win seats in elections must navigate a political labyrinth full of vipers" and a "mongrel parliament", hence "the only reason to go into that body is with the aim of gutting it"[62]. Indeed, the major political parties constituted, according to NA, "an ensemble of immoral criminal misfits and paedophiles"[63]. However, according to NA, the idea that democracy is a dead-end did not necessarily mean that the route to power was forever foreclosed because NA maintained that fascists may succeed without fully engaging in the electoral process.

As NA explained, the basic political lesson of the fascist movements of the 1920s and '30s was that "in some instances power was acquired with only a minority of the public affiliating with what could be termed fascistic groups", consequently the key to the success of these organisations was simple, "quality over quantity"[64]. The message was straightforward and seductively simple — democracy could, and should, be circumvented.

Of course, the fascist conception of the State is explicitly authoritarian because it is assumed that the masses love strength and despise weakness. A strong State is advocated by fascists as a quasi-ethical manifestation of the national will. It should therefore be the focus of ultimate authority and possess the coercive power that reflects its significance as protector of the national community. However, the contemporary British State was seen by NA as desperately weak, feeble and directionless. Nevertheless, fascists still needed to use the State for their own purposes, as NA believed: "Our ultimate aim can only ever be achieved through State power and the complicity of State institutions such as Police, Army, Intelligence Services etc"[65]. So ultimately the State should be used to pursue certain overriding political objectives, particularly with regard to race (see later). We can certainly assume that, under a neo-Nazi dispensation, the notion of civil freedom (as understood by liberal theorists) would be rendered redundant, and individual human rights subordinated to the "will of the people" as dictated by the fascist party, an organisation designed specifically to mobilise the masses.

The society over which the fascist State presides is inevitably hierarchical and disciplined to comply with certain values and facilitate social cohesion. This was very much reflected in the NA position: "It is a fact of existence that hierarchy is innate — which we don't deny, but in the people's State every citizen has an allotted responsibility ... and is valued as such"[66].

However, some members of society would be explicitly excluded from this crude functionalist arrangement, for example disabled people and homosexuals. National Action referred to anyone with a physical or mental disability in the most derisory and dismissive terms as "nature's rejects" and exclaimed the need to re-introduce Section 28 (1988), part of a Local Government Act which prohibited the promotion of homosexual activity. Evidently NA viewed homosexuality as "degenerate" and was keen to re-introduce legal discrimination against the gay community[67]. Similarly, female rights and equal worth were only considered legitimate by NA in the context of genetic reproduction and securing a future for the white race (see later)[68]. For NA, nationalism required that the State focus on building a more integrated community by emphasising the social, cultural and aesthetic needs of the "indigenous" ethnic majority, whilst deviation from State-imposed social values should not be tolerated under any circumstances[69].

However, as with the classical fascist movements, there was ambiguity in NA literature surrounding the role that the State ought to play in the field of economics. National Action had nothing resembling a coherent economic plan and no genuine analysis beyond vague aspirations to eliminate usury and the so-called "creditor class". Although there was an occasional nod in the direction of the idea of Social Credit as developed by C.H. Douglas and Arthur Kitson, which was originally intended to eradicate "debt slavery", there was no detailed economic policy programme[70].

There was, however, some facile sloganising about the need for a concerted effort to undermine the "global financial system" which, it was claimed, eroded national purpose and identity[71]. Furthermore, in more general terms, capitalism was seen as an economic system that puts profit and production before the people, who were merely "cogs in a great and merciless money-making machine"[72]. Indeed National Action maintained that a variety of serious social pathologies, such as demographic disaster, atomisation, crime and degeneracy, existed because of the unrestrained free enterprise system, saying "the catalyst for these pathogens in our national body is the capitalist system"[73]. Most significantly, the free movement of labour was seen as the logical consequence of an unfettered capitalist economic system. The British worker could not possibly compete with those willing to toil for meagre wages, therefore the essence of capitalism and globalisation, according to NA, is that they facilitate more extensive exploitation. As a consequence of this perspective NA asserted that "we are the real leaders of the class struggle", because "the left is led by the middle-class people" and "dealing with immigration will help poorer communities — one day we hope to eradicate the relevance of class"[74]. It is evident that, from the NA perspective, economics could not be divorced from the more significant mission-critical political priorities of the fascist State: "It is true that if we do not understand economics then we cannot understand the full significance of the racial struggle, however what would be the point of any political or economic reform if it is not specifically for the maintenance and life of the race"[75]. According to NA, economics should be subordinated to other far more important ideological requirements, particularly the survival of the white race.

Of course, when analysing fascism, it is impossible to avoid the notion of race which is absolutely central to Nazism and the key component of its ideology. In terms of historical experience fascism constituted a political praxis that prioritised race, and was predicated on the implementation of racist "solutions" to political, social and economic problems. In classical versions of fascism there was always a qualitative distinction to be made between those advocating cultural supremacism, and those committed to a more instrumental genetic version of racism. Mussolini's Italian fascists were, for the most part, exponents of a racism which was underscored by notions of culture in terms of national history, language, values and traditions, whilst Hitler's Nazis emphasised a racial hierarchy that was based on the importance of biology and bloodline. National Action was unquestionably more favourably disposed toward the latter position. It was this key issue of race that saw NA at its most vituperative and vitriolic.

The NA website had the tagline "For a free white Britain" and explicitly advocated white supremacy. It would not be an exaggeration to suggest that NA, like all other Nazi organisations, was obsessed with eugenics and the need to ensure the purity of the Aryan race. This aim was forcefully and unapologetically articulated: "National Action is committed to a White Britain" and "it is the uncontroversial and sincerely held belief of all National Action members that there will be a race war in Britain and the whites are going to win it"[76]. The NA website elaborated: "Our views are widely held but not consistently applied, people express their racism by voting for UKIP which we think is unhealthy. Our country will not be saved by cowards who mince their words with horse shit"[77]. Here the often quoted words of racist ideologue David Lane assume a seminal significance: "We must secure the existence of our people and a future for white children"[78]. As pro-NA fascist ideologue Fenek Solere explains: "National Action understands a Nation is in the blood of a people, in the land those people occupy, and the culture that blood creates. Race is not a social construct. Society is a racial construct .. .so long as the blood remains pure, Europeans can overcome anything"[79]. However, different ethnicities inhabiting the same geographical space and competing for "essential resources" such as "land, food, water, wealth and women" would, NA claimed, lead inevitably to social conflict and even national disaster because "multiculturalism is a code-word for White Genocide"[80].

The "white race" was viewed by NA as the origin of civilisation and the source of all major technological advance, and these conclusions were drawn straight from the conceptual repertoire of Nazi sociobiology: "We know race does to some extent dictate one's character and ability to fit in to, add value to, and abide by the rules of a civilised community"[81]. Furthermore, "some behaviour and characteristics are racially ingrained and despite our best attempts to correct them haven't, can't and won't change. You can take the African out of Africa but it doesn't take the African out of him — he has the same inherited mentality and behaviour as his ancestors, in the same way that we do too"[82]. For NA cultural superiority was therefore seen as an immutable sociobiological fact. Given the existence of this undeniable genetic hierarchy "black culture" was persistently disparaged by NA and compared to the finest in "white" cultural achievement, as reflected in the works of, for instance, Shakespeare and Mozart[83]. Indeed, it was asserted by NA that black people had a low average IQ, were particularly prone to engage in criminal activity (especially rape) and were liable to cheat the welfare system. Hence hostility to those who do not "belong" in the "national community" was ubiquitous in NA literature: "White children are brutalised and intimidated on a daily basis, year in and year out, and forced to live alongside savages"[84]. Indeed, NA asserted that "the illegitimate offspring of the tent wandering troglodytes" were invading Europe, and NA also claimed (without evidence) that a white European woman was raped every 4.8 seconds by an immigrant: "Our enemy will use sperm alongside bullets to further his cause"[85]. However, according to NA, "although it would be disingenuous to suggest that we feel no malice toward those who have come to this country seeking personal gain, at our expense … our real anger lies with those who let them come in the first place"[86]. In short, the prevailing liberal consensus on immigration precipitated a perceived "immigration crisis", and the creators of multicultural orthodoxy were the primary target of NA opprobrium.

This overt racist animosity towards immigrants, including refugees and asylum seekers, was obviously powerfully reinforced by the consequences of the so-called "war on terror" and the underlying Islamophobia that exists in certain sections of British society. As NA put it "they have flushed the toilet and the excrement of the East is flowing West"[87]. As far as NA was concerned, "psychotic Islamic militants" were intent on territorial expansion and enslaving people, while Europe was importing "millions" of adherents to an "alien desert religion"[88]. From such a perspective, any dialogue with Muslims was seen as fundamentally misguided because it would culminate "in the inevitable call for the black rag of Islam to fly from public buildings and demands for further Mosque construction"[89]. In essence, as far as NA was concerned, Muslims were engaged in a take-over bid for Europe and Britain was being "swamped by non-assimilated illiterates who still find time between their prayers to procreate in order to collect even more child benefit and better housing, while all the time pushing for the interests of their own race before that of their over-generous hosts"[90]. All immigrants, especially Muslims, were portrayed by NA in the most dismissive and disparaging terms possible.

National Action thus declared that "the only important criteria for the future people's State is that you are a member of a united national community"[91]. Indeed NA promoted the White Independent Nation movement, which aimed to develop white-only enclaves within the UK. However, it is important to note that from a NA viewpoint, many fellow Europeans were also considered to be, essentially, of "white" heritage. So the petty parochial nationalism of the "little England" perspective was explicitly rejected by NA because the "island mentality" needed to change in order to embrace a broader conception of white European ethnicity[92]. Although the "white race" might be beset with extraordinary challenges, the Nazis in National Action were banking on their assumption that the desire to protect territory, and the survival instinct, remained hard-wired within "white" racial and ethnic identity. In the meantime, the catastrophic consequences of failure to protect and promulgate the white race were contrasted with the utopia that awaited a successful nationalist movement: "It is the white race who see all meaning and reason to live in this world, without them everything would be lost. If we win, then we get a second chance. We will start a civilisation that will one day be perfect, where everyone is white, happy, healthy and intelligent — they will be biological gods"[93].

In practical terms, the actual mechanisms and processes necessary for achieving this white wonderland remained obscure and NA remained obstinately opaque regarding the specific details, but occasionally the florid rhetoric afforded a glimpse of what might be in store, should NA ever have been in a position to influence events: "If it is possible for us to take power, as we believe, then the most desirable and effective way of dealing with the race problem is for it to be carried out through civil and legislative institutions — the arms of the State" but "involuntary repatriation or 'ethnic cleansing' is not without precedent"[94]. Such sentiments were bound to induce anxiety in anyone with the most cursory knowledge of contemporary European history.

Of course Nazi notions of race and racism are most intimately connected to the idea of anti-Semitism. The experience of anti-Semitism was central to Nazi ideology and, given the Holocaust, it represents the most significant and graphic aspect of its practical historical impact. National Action was vehemently anti-Semitic: "For National Action, open anti-Semitism is the ultimate marker of being a good, authentic nationalist"[95]. As NA pointed out, "to be on 'our side' a nationalist must be openly racist and openly anti-Semitic"[96]. Moreover, "weakness on the Jewish question is simply unforgivable, ignorance is inexcusable, the Jew has a name and it glares you in the face when discussing any world problems"[97]. The influence of Judaism was seen everywhere and in practically every aspect of political life, even the UK Independence Party was referred to as "Jewkip", a "kosher party" and NA activists were distinctly unimpressed by the existence of a "Jewish Division" in the anti-Islam street organisation the English Defence League[98]. In NA literature there was constant reference to the Zionist

Occupation Government (ZOG) and the Jewish dominance of finance, academia and the entertainment industry[99]. One world ("anti-national") organisations like the World Trade Organisation (WTO), International Monetary Fund (IMF) and the United Nations (UN) were seen as reflecting direct Jewish dominance at the global political and policy making level[100].

So obsessed was NA with the ubiquitous impact of their racial nemesis that all the familiar anti-Semitic tropes were deployed about banking and finance. Indeed, according to NA, Jews were even said to control the porn industry in an effort to subvert the morals of gentiles, and they were believed to be somehow responsible for the narcotics trade, gambling and crime[101]. National Action argued that the Jews also encouraged immigration through an emphasis on social inclusion and tolerance because ultimately Judaism seeks an end to Christian Europe, meanwhile the State of Israel and other "Zionist" forces were said to be able to cynically manipulate the rest of the world for their own nefarious purposes[102]. Needless to say, NA paid particular attention to, and promoted, those sources that have engaged in Holocaust denial, in effect all accounts that see the Shoah as, essentially, a hoax or a myth[103]. The practical consequence of this blatantly anti-Semitic perspective was entirely predictable and clearly articulated by NA: "It is with glee that we will enact the final solution across Europe — that will be justice"[104]. Genocide, as the logical, practical outcome of a Nazi ideology consistently applied, was accepted with alacrity by National Action.

Obviously fascism was designed, to a significant extent, to destroy communism and cleanse "the nation" of all of its subversive internal enemies[105]. All the familiar negations that appeared in classical fascism, reappear in NA discourse. According to NA the spurious ideals of liberty, equality and fraternity led directly to a variety of "blood-soaked despots masquerading under the guise of egalitarianism", whilst Marxism was perceived as little more than a tawdry Jewish plot[106]. In fact NA claimed "Marxism, the purported 'economic theory', was never anything more than a social vision to destroy civilisation given an economic basis by the Jew Karl Marx"[107], and without the Jews there would have been no Bolshevism (even Lenin was considered a Jew by NA as a consequence of one Jewish grandparent!). However, NA opined that "despite the economic science of the right being a thousand times superior and credible to that of the left, the right wingers are regularly beaten by modern day adherents of (rebranded) Marxism", in effect "your average left activist is sub-human and anti-social, yet they run this society through default — because they are not challenged"[108]. It is therefore important to note that, from an NA point of view, any notion of political transcendence that is designed to improve society is destined for ultimate failure: "What has always made the state a hell on earth has been precisely that man has tried to make it his heaven"[109].

However, although NA focused much of its rage against the left, it is crucial to understand that it attempted to portray itself as defying conventional categorisation in terms of the traditional left-right ideological axis. This is because NA saw capitalism and communism as essentially part of the same global economic system. As NA explained: "Capitalism is, in everyday discussion synonymous with the so-called political 'right'. This has been an unfortunate burden for any political force on the 'right' that has attempted to represent a truly national outlook. For precisely this reason, National Action has attempted to present itself as both nationalist and socialist — as a means of differentiating ourselves from the rest of the political spectrum; both right and left"[110]. Hence National Action eschewed the more conventional political labels and claimed to exist in a vector which orthodox ideological mapping was unable to locate because mankind is not reducible to an economic algorithm or a pawn in the class war. As far as NA was concerned, "capitalism and communism are two sides of the same shekel. Both tools of the pig System and the internationalists' agenda"[111]. Hence NA asserted that ultimately "the true partisan of the future will offer resistance to the homogenized, global, technological civilisation labouring under the iron fist of egalitarianism'"[112]. It is therefore crucial to note that National Action's version of "socialism" should not be confused with any notions of social justice or equality, as they affirmed: "We will fight for white Socialism"[113]. The ideology of NA might plausibly be described as collectivist in the sense that they have an ideology constructed on a conception of the (white ethnic) social group (rather than individual or class), but they certainly cannot be characterised as "socialist" in any meaningful way since they explicitly and vehemently reject (various) universal notions of equality (civil, political, social, and/or economic) which form the essence of any genuinely socialist endeavour.

As a consequence of this brief survey it is absolutely clear that National Action's ideology was self-evidently and unapologetically fascist and Nazi: romantic anti-rationalism, social Darwinism, aggressive nationalism (xenophobia), along with an emphasis on an authoritarian State and a disciplined society, the need for assertive dictatorial leadership, and a vague idea of a "third way" beyond communism and capitalism, were combined with an adherence to cultural/sociobiological racism — with a heavy emphasis on anti-Semitism. All of these features appeared prominently in NA literature and the group were, without question, fanatical exponents of the classical paradigm of Nazism, as outlined by Adolf Hitler[114].

The true nature of British Nazism, and some uncomfortable truths

Although the ideological template was provided by classical forms of fascism (eg. Germany and Italy between 1922-45) and therefore National Action can be legitimately described as an authentic organisational embodiment of Nazi ideology, its political praxis also clearly complied with the tradition of fascism in Britain. The infamous triptych of the British Union of Fascists (BUF), National Front (NF), and British National Party (BNP) were all manifestations of the fascist experience set in a specifically British context although they also acquired their underlying ideological impetus from the ideas which animated the classical fascist movements and regimes on the continent. Each of these organisations, in its own way, kept fascist ideas alive in Britain during onerous circumstances and in its own, albeit nanoscopic way, NA was simply attempting to perform precisely the same political task[115].

So it is important to recognise that NA is very much an integral component of a British political tradition which is represented by the likes of Arnold Leese, Colin Jordan, John Tyndall and, more recently, Nick Griffin. Indeed, in terms of more specific ideological, strategic and tactical emphasis, there are some more obvious and specific domestic resonances. For instance, NA itself praised the BUF as the most significant practical example of fascist politics on the far right, and the virulent, almost pathological, anti-Semitism of NA is redolent of examples like the Imperial Fascist League in the 1930s or National Socialist Movement in the 1960s. There are also some similarities with BUF leader Oswald Mosley's ideas, as articulated during his post-war Union Movement phase when he stressed the common heritage of Europeans and the "sacred flame" of "Europe a Nation"[116]. Perhaps still more significant are the clear parallels to be drawn with the strategy of "tension and terror" as outlined and developed by the National Front in the 1980s[117]. During this period there were those in the NF who had been attracted by the Terza Posizione of the Strasser brothers Gregor and Otto, and they aimed to reinvigorate the nationalist cause via a new caste of "political soldiers" who would defend white culture against the "barbarian hordes"[118]. The NF's obsession with social disorder and rebirth indicated a clear belief in the cathartic re-calibration of human nature through violence, indeed the "political soldiers" became increasingly fixated by the idea of armed insurrection, after which the nationalist phoenix would arise out of the ashes of the old, decadent and decaying democratic society. This shift toward clandestine subversion and the use of violence was also reflected in the NF's organisational contacts with pro-state Protestant paramilitary groups in Ulster and the neo-fascist Nuclei Armati Rivoluzionari (NAR) in Italy. The resonances with the NA's belief in "leaderless resistance" and the tactical utility of terror are unmistakable.

Similarly, the NA emphasis on street-level activism and confrontation also has a discernible domestic fascist heritage, with distinctive echoes in recent fascist history in Britain. It was Nick Griffin who, in deploying classic fascist tactics, proclaimed that it was far more important to control the streets than the council chambers, and who aimed to do so with "well directed boots and fists". A comparable effort to "control the streets" was attempted by Combat 18, which was formed by the BNP as a protection squad against left-wing activists who had achieved some significant successes in disrupting the party's activities[119]. Despite the pavement posturing reminiscent of contemporaneous football "firms" (and the extraordinary moral panic this precipitated in the British media), C18 never actually fulfilled its paramilitary pretensions. The BNP was, in effect, forced to "de-commission the boot" (as Nick Griffin and Tony Lecomber put it) due to the assiduous attention of groups like Anti-Fascist Action[120]. Eventually C18 was jettisoned by the BNP in 1994 as a State-infiltrated embarrassment, after which an electoral strategy was deployed in a populist effort to embrace political respectability. Combat 18 subsequently degenerated into a drinking club for drug dealers and Hitler-worshipping fantasists. In actual fact National Action effectively acknowledged that it was itself formed, at least in part, as a reaction to this failure to control public space in the face of sustained anti-fascist resistance, as NA themselves confirmed: "National Action was formed in the face of adversity, in hate of the red terror that humbled and fell so many Nationalist groups before us"[121]. Indeed, NA argued that "any group who is not working to actively combat these thugs is a non-starter because the group either gets suppressed, or they must self-marginalise their own activities to places where they have no effect", therefore "we must first break the red terror"[122]. So NA was, in some ways, merely the latest effort to respond to the success anti-fascist organisations have had in confronting fascists in Britain[123]. Despite its lofty ideological pretensions, NA was not so much the harbinger of a new national "revolution", but the bitter bile produced after the fascist far right had digested the fact that they had been comprehensively defeated on the streets.

That NA is very much a part of the fascist tradition in Britain might be axiomatic, but it is also worth noting that they also had much broader influences as well, partly because of the fact that they emphasised the need for a pan-European perspective. As a result NA had links with a variety of far right organisations such as National Rebirth of Poland (NOP), Sigud and the Nordic Resistance Movement, White Rex and Wotan Jugend. There is also evidence of some contact with the Ukrainian paramilitary group Azov Division and the Anti-Kapitalist Kollective in Germany. Moreover, National Action was inspired by the recent "success" of far-right organisations which have made a significant impact in Europe, such as the Jobbik movement in Hungary, and Golden Dawn in Greece, which provided an example that "glitters tantalizingly on the horizon", indeed NA admitted that "Golden Dawn in Greece are a perfect example of what we'd like to replicate"[124]. It is also possible to discern other, more esoteric, ideological and historical inspirations from Europe, such as the authoritarian impulses of Primo de Rivera and the Spanish Falange, Codreanu's Romanian Iron Guard, or the anti-rational mysticism of Julius Evola. Indeed, given the fact that NA had set itself a much wider cultural remit, a more pertinent and contemporary comparator might be Casa Pound in Italy, which began as a squatter organisation but developed into a social network in the Esquilino district of Rome. Thereafter Casa Pound managed to spread outward to other cities, and boasted a theatre company, a journal, as well as radio and television outlets. Leaders, like Gianluca Iannone, who presided over a "circle of fighters" operated in the style of Mussolini's squadristi, whilst expressing love for the "Fatherland"[125].

Furthermore, it should be recognised that the increasingly globalised and interconnected nature of the world undoubtedly helps groups like NA develop new relationships with like-minded individuals and organisations, which has in turn precipitated dramatic changes in the scope and relevance of the broader "imagined" community of fascist activists[126]. In this context the internet has proven to be an important technological mechanism through which to disseminate Nazi ideas. Websites provide easy accessibility across national borders, and the internet facilitates direct contact between fascist ideologues in a way hardly imaginable to previous generations. Access to a plethora of explicitly Nazi ideas has never been easier. NA obviously aimed to exploit this facility to the fullest possible extent before its activities drew the attention of the British security services. Irrespective of recent developments, and the demise of National Action, fascist radicalisation is now an integral part of an evolving cyber sub-culture that identifies and attacks ideological enemies while gaining strength and impetus from contact with other entities with shared political values.

Although inspiration, in fascist terms, was drawn from a multifarious and eclectic range of domestic and international sources, the significance of NA (and other similar groups) might nevertheless lie in the fact that it has been able to sustain such ideas at all. As Jackson argues: "To comment on their small scale as an inherent indication of their political failure misses the point: groupuscules often view developing a sense of authenticity and commitment among a small band of activists as a core aim"[127]. In fact NA was "trying to carve out a distinct profile for itself, framing its activities as provocative and extreme"[128] and in this way, by turning style into substance, the group aimed to keep the tradition of fascism alive and provide impetus for other like-minded elements. National Action offered "a small handful of activists an old set of reference points that (were) set out in a new, dynamic manner. The aim (was) to connect young people with an extreme past, and make it seem relevant for the present day"[129]. The unique selling point for National Action was a combination of its youthful, modern appearance, along with the adoption of high-profile, provocative methods, whilst nevertheless adhering steadfastly to traditional Nazi politics. In this sense "success" for the ideological Nazis is a strictly relative phenomenon, and the mere existence of such organisations constitutes a victory for them of sorts.

In fact Jackson raises another aspect of NA ideology which needs to be explicitly addressed, because he makes the assertion that NA's political aims were/are ultimately "nothing less than a revolution overthrowing the liberal democratic order"[130]. Here it might be argued that Jackson is simply articulating a commonly held belief, indeed many academics, journalists and commentators have stressed the "revolutionary" nature of fascist ideology and the potentially transformative impact of fascism in practice. There is no doubt that NA activists would concur with such an assessment, as NA put it: "The only way we can ever win is with a conscious revolution...and our idea of revolution is one where heads roll"[131]. This all sounds very dramatic and the exponents of NA's specific manifestation of Nazism unquestionably saw their ideology as a revolutionary creed: "The right, if it is to win, must become a revolution — an open conspiracy to topple the system … we fight for a Britain that is both nationalist and socialist, we fight for a revolution"[132]. From this perspective, Nazi nationalism, in rejecting the "materialism" of both capitalism and communism, constitutes a commitment to the full-scale "revolutionary" transformation of society.

However, the idea that fascism is a revolutionary ideology should be treated with considerable circumspection given historical experience. In fact, Hitler's version of Nazism had emphatically rejected the more radical social vision of Anton Drexler, the Strasser brothers and the other "third positionists" at the Nazi's Bamberg conference in 1926, long before he was invited to take control of Germany in 1933. The neutralisation of radical elements was decisively concluded in 1934 with the so-called "Night of the Long Knives". Hitler was thus anxious to divert the dangerous forces of political discontent toward the safer terrain of social order and stability. Certainly it might be argued that fascism precipitates a radical, even "revolutionary" political transformation from democracy to dictatorship, with drastic implications for civil liberties, ethnic minorities and organised labour, but it is crucial to understand that the underlying hierarchical structure of society remains fundamentally unaltered. In essence, despite the florid rhetoric and posturing, fascist ideology *in practice* has been about preserving the prevailing socio-economic structures rather than attempting to precipitate a radical restructuring of social relations. In many ways fascism was the reaction against those seeking a genuine and irreversible transformation of society. Indeed, fascism was, in Joachim Fest's famous phrase, "a revolt on behalf of order", and whatever the political pretensions of miniscule Nazi groups like National Action, this has been the reactionary reality of fascism. Fascism stages the spectacle of "revolution" in order to protect and preserve the capitalist system which is based on class division and exploitation.

In reality fascism is far closer to conservatism as a political ideology — there is a clear and identifiable family resemblance. Indeed, in Britain, prior to 1939, fascism was widely seen as a more muscular articulation of essentially conservative ideas. Fear of Bolshevism and the possible consequences of the extension of the franchise precipitated a shared anxiety about the trajectory of society and the need for order. The first explicitly fascist organisation in Britain, the British Fascisti (BF) formed in 1923, urged its supporters to vote Conservative, and the BF's "blueshirts" even provided security at Conservative Party meetings. In fact, prior to the war, many members of the British ruling class expressed admiration for fascist ideas and noted the various "achievements" of fascist regimes. Indeed both Hitler and Mussolini were often viewed as bulwarks of civilisation against the evils of Asiatic communism. Certain sections of the British upper classes not only flirted shamelessly with fascism before 1939, many conservatives saw fascism as simply a more virile and robust expression of their own political perspective. The reality is that there is no impenetrable ideological firewall separating fascism from the apparently more mundane ideas of conservatism. Indeed, in some ways the focus on the caricature villains of the fascist "other", with their swastikas and overt anti-Semitism, enables society to ignore some of its own imperfections and may actually obscure the actual nature of the relationship between conservatism and fascism which is far more ambiguous than conventional wisdom suggests.

This point is worth developing because a kind of anti-fascist myth exists, particularly in Britain, as a consequence of the war. The uncomfortable fact is that from a British policy-making perspective the war against Hitler (and Mussolini) reflected a desire to protect certain long-held strategic, geopolitical and economic interests, rather than a conflict over ideological principle or morality. The British ruling class was drawn into an anti-fascist position by the foreign policy of Hitler, which posed a tangible threat to Britain's material interests, rather than reflecting any deeply held antipathy toward fascist ideology. Even the Conservative Party's own "anti-fascist" warlord, Winston Churchill, is on record as expressing his admiration for both Hitler and Mussolini, and the dullards in the royal family would have undoubtedly supplied their very own Quisling or Petain, if the war had gone badly. The collaborators would undoubtedly have come predominantly from the conservative elites and the Establishment. So, in effect, the war in the West represented a conflict of interests rather than ideas (in contrast to the ideological war of annihilation in the East) and it was a conflict conducted primarily against fascists rather than fascism. This dimension of the conflagration has, of course, been distorted by post-war reaction to the Holocaust, which revealed the evil essence of Nazism and precipitated a retrospective rationalisation by conservative elements in Britain. This revision may have been an understandable reflex in response to the grotesque reality of genocide, but it should not be allowed to obfuscate the real nature of the relationship between conservatism, the ruling class and fascism. It is always worth remembering that it was Margaret Thatcher who called Nelson Mandela a "terrorist" and feted the vile dictator Pinochet. Essentially, conservatism and fascism are cut from the same ideological cloth and fascism is, in practice, old-fashioned reactionary conservatism on steroids.

Fascism is therefore a right-wing conservative, reactionary, anti-working class ideology and, despite all the radical (pre-system) rhetoric of "revolution", its social function has always been to defend the capitalist economic system during a period of prolonged socio-economic crisis. Fascism occurs when there is a possibility that political democracy might actually put economic democracy on the agenda, and in that case the former is destroyed by ideological fanatics who, in effect, have an identity of interest with those people who possess wealth and power.

This does not mean fascists pose no threat to those elites, that would be an overly reductive conclusion — it is an uneasy, quasi-functional symbiosis because there is an autonomous ideological dynamic that drives the fascist movement and which poses a distinct threat to social elites. However, all the historical evidence suggests that fascists have been perfectly happy to accommodate capitalism, and its concomitant social relations[133]. In fact fascism is a permanent, albeit relatively autonomous manifestation, of capitalist development itself, and it is always capable of achieving success when the ruling class is not able to manage the consequences of socio-economic crises effectively and are therefore prepared to make a desperate deal in order to drag the nation away from the abyss. It is worth noting the historical fact that those fascists who were successful did not actually storm the ramparts of State power — the drawbridge was lowered from within by conservative elites who were willing to risk an accommodation with a movement of ideological fanatics, for its own purposes, in order to destroy the organised working class. In effect a bargain is struck between the prevailing ruling class, which is willing to relinquish its political power in order to retain its economic predominance. This was a phenomenon that Marx identified many years ago with regard to Bonapartism — the bourgeoisie is, on occasion, prepared to relinquish its Crown in order to save its purse.

This also relates to another critical point of interpretation. Matthew Collins argues that National Action set itself up as a "pure national socialist movement with a mission to sweep aside the old morally corrupted organisations but, of course, its followers are more interested in crude racism, anti-Semitism and violence. *As a result, the threat from NA is less political than physical*" (italics added)[134]. This observation, although pertinent, is overdrawn for two reasons: firstly, fascism is an ideology expressed "in action" so the distinction between theory and practice is not entirely straightforward; secondly, and more importantly, the political ideology itself may be far more dangerous than Collins assumes, and here we come to yet another very uncomfortable truth.

The threat from fascist doctrine lies essentially in the fact that it provides an overriding sense of purpose, and it is also a credo that is actually capable of supplying (albeit spurious) explanations for social decay, deprivation and alienation. This ideology facilitates a desire to belong and promotes the idea of personal self-sacrifice for a noble cause. Nazism is unquestionably viewed by its adherents as a form of mission or political religion, as NA activist Raymond exclaimed: "What we are doing is Holy"[135]. This fact is vitally important in an unstable era when people yearn for certainty. So the sense of "sanctified" devotion and dedication generated by such an ideology should not be summarily dismissed or under-estimated because fascism does provide "answers". Of course, sentiments outlining the importance of a "sacred mission" may constitute, at one level, a facile self-justification for social prejudice, but such conviction is only fanciful if one assumes a static socio-economic context where such notions are marginalised in perpetuity by an over-riding liberal consensus. Unfortunately there is no doubt that the Nazi brand is capable of being re-packaged once again, and circumstances can change dramatically — so much so, in fact, that fascism may not always be seen as the most unattractive and least credible product in the market place of political ideas.

Now this tentative observation relates to an even more disturbing aspect of fascism which will undoubtedly unsettle the liberal intellectuals who tend to study such things. Nazi ideology is threatening and dangerous precisely because, to certain sections of the (white) working class, it can offer a far more satisfying and convincing credo than the austere individualism that underpins neoliberalism. This assertion requires careful elaboration. Fascism can be attractive because it is a form of collectivism, which aims to transcend a sterile economic orthodoxy which focuses on the instrumental importance of the autonomous individual whose value is determined solely by a capacity to consume goods and services in the free market. One of the fundamental insights of fascist ideology was (is) the emphasis on the social dimension and its acknowledgement that people need to feel a sense of belonging. Fascists know that there is more to existence than economic consumption. The pursuit of a much vaunted "liberty" in capitalist societies often constitutes the endorsement of policies that, while unleashing private enterprise, nevertheless forces ordinary people to become alienated and cast adrift in the free market wilderness. Given the recent trajectory of economic decline in many capitalist societies, for a growing number of people the actual material benefits of individual market-based freedoms are becoming far less obvious. The fascists claim to be able to take everyone, minus the "other", to a better life, and this kind of rhetoric resonates in marginalised communities where, in recent years, progressive political aspirations have been seriously attenuated. The plain fact is that during difficult periods desperate people will seize on anything to provide an "explanation" for their predicament and a prospect of respite. The sense of purpose, devotion and dedication provided by fascist ideology, and the inspiration that this can provide, should therefore not be disregarded. Hence the Nazi ideal, desperate and dystopian though it undoubtedly is, nevertheless reflects an impulse to accommodate a collective consciousness which transcends existential atomisation and gives human existence a greater meaning — people may gravitate toward a movement that is capable of giving their lives a larger significance.

Anti-fascist resistance, and the failure of the liberal left

Of course, in such a context, resistance to such organisations is absolutely imperative and the exponents of fascism need to be confronted both ideologically and physically. However, such a militant, pro-active approach to fascist organisations has been the subject of some considerable controversy recently with eminent intellectual Noam Chomsky questioning the utility of robust physical resistance against the (proto-fascist) Alt-Right in the USA[136]. Similarly, Slavoj Zizek, whilst stating clearly that fascism is the consequence of a failure on the left, has nevertheless insisted that antifascist violence is little more than "panicky posturing"[137]. Indeed, elsewhere Zizek has been far more explicit in his condemnation of physical force resistance to fascism, arguing that anti-fascists should not use violence against Nazis: "If a guy talks like that jerk (Richard Spencer), you should just ignore him. If he hits you turn around. Don't even acknowledge him as a person … slapping him is too much of a recognition. You should treat him or her or whoever as a nonperson, literally"[138]. When leftist academics of such calibre and status call into question the use of violence, it is as well to consider quite carefully the arguments at hand.

Obviously some of the perspectives that reject the notion of robust anti-fascist resistance can be extremely powerful and persuasive. For example, there is the idea that the use of violence has some kind of pre-figurative dimension and should therefore be dismissed as a viable tactic. This position stresses that violence often precipitates more of the same, and is often connected to the related notion that the use of physical resistance inevitably leads to the deployment of methods which are indistinguishable from the enemy being opposed. In this way critics often conflate fascism and militant anti-fascism as possessing essentially the same, inherently violent, characteristics. There are, of course, some other very strong arguments which can and have been utilised against militant anti-fascist activists, and these tend to prioritise civil liberties and the right to freedom of speech. This is essentially the belief that fascist ideas can and should be exposed to the penetrating light of democratic debate. Rational and reasonable people will, it is claimed, see through the lies and malevolent half-truths of fascist discourse and be convinced of the intellectual rigour of those advocating tolerance, freedom and human dignity.

However, such arguments should not deflect anti-fascists who prioritise a combination of methods. To take the free speech arguments first. To prioritise liberal freedoms above political realities would be a fundamental mistake. We know, from historical experience, that fascists only ever use democracy in order to destroy it — although they are perfectly willing to milk the Parliamentary cow before it gets butchered. Fascists cynically use freedom of speech and democracy in order to demolish them. Moreover, freedom of speech is, in effect, a contingent liberty, and cannot be construed as an absolute right in all circumstances, and much depends upon the precise political circumstances and social consequences. We all accept conventional constraints on our freedom of speech in the interest of respecting individual sensibilities or indeed for the common good, and some of these restrictions happen to be enshrined in law. No-one would seriously support the right of paedophiles to argue in favour of sex with children, or misogynists the freedom to debate the merits of raping women. Constraints on ideological fascists are therefore legitimate because in practice fascism leads inexorably toward dictatorship, coercion, concentration camps and genocide. We know this. In any case, Nazis do not possess the kind of moral or ethical framework with which it is possible to engage purposefully or productively, and liberal attempts to expose the "truth" will never puncture the fascist desire for domination — it is not always possible to render a fascist harmless by the persuasive power of sophisticated arguments. (However, such a "no platform" position does not mean that it is wise to let the State impose its own restrictions on fascist activities, as we shall see).

To focus on the methods utilised by anti-fascist activists, and to prioritise means rather than ends, is yet another categorical error. Anti-fascists living in working class areas often have to deal with the very real threat of fascism in their communities. Given the historical and theoretical reality of fascism and Nazism, ordinary people in working class communities, where fascists try to incubate their grotesque ideology, have every right to resist because they have most to lose. Indeed, given that fascism constitutes a clear and present danger to working class communities, and the fact that trade unionists, socialists, communists and anarchists will be the first to inhabit the fascist concentration camps, resistance to it becomes a moral obligation, by all means necessary. Pontificating from a relatively safe distance has always been the prerogative of scholarly elites, and academics do not tend to live in working-class communities — so maybe the difficult decision to physically resist should be accorded a little more respect. "Fighting fascism" is not a facile slogan or a figure of speech to be frivolously deployed in faculty seminars — it is a practical reality and an unfortunate necessity. However, there is absolutely no equivalence between the violence of fascism and anti-fascism, despite what some academics might suggest, and in some circumstances the ends really do justify the means — what else could?

Fascism therefore is the political equivalent of plutonium, and there is no genuinely safe means to engage with it. A "no platform" position with regard to overtly fascist organisations intent on violent and aggressive expansion is entirely legitimate, and force is, on occasion, a viable and necessary option. This fact has been confirmed by the British experience of anti-fascism, which has been successful in challenging fascists for the control of public space. Indeed it is interesting to note that it was militant, street level anti-fascist activists who did most of the heavy lifting when confronting the British Union of Fascists in the 1930s, the National Front in the 1970s and the BNP in the 1980s and '90s[139]. Physical force, used as a tactic rather than a principle, was used very effectively to confront and deter those organisations trying to intimidate and divide people in those local communities where fascists tried to disseminate their repulsive ideas.

For those opposing fascism from within their own communities, violence is not a reflection of some Sorellian working class catharsis or a meaningless expression of hyper-masculinity, it is a straightforward and simple means of self-defence. Violence is always a weapon of last resort, but when faced with ideological Nazis who have absolutely no intention of engaging with the electoral process or respecting democratic structures or processes, then the precise and proportionate deployment of physical resistance is entirely appropriate. Robust resistance is, at times, the only viable currency and no serious commentator on political affairs could possibly suggest that the physical protest conducted on Cable Street in 1936 was illegitimate, and anyone who doubts the contemporary utility of such a tactic would do well to consider the comments made recently by US academic and activist Cornel West after the white supremacist murder of Heather Meyer at a rally in Charlottesville in 2017. In certain very specific circumstances, force may be the *only* means of asserting our right, as an unconditional necessity, to defend ourselves (and humanity) against barbarism.

In fact there is a broader observation to be made here because in many ways there is an obvious blind spot on the left when it comes to the use of force. This point is easily illustrated with reference to the resistance deployed against the evil apartheid regime in South Africa. "Leftists" who fawn over the memory of Nelson Mandela and the African National Congress conveniently forget that he was a founder member of the armed wing, Umkhontho We Sizwe. Indeed, some of those on the liberal left (especially in the Labour Party) have been guilty of the most asinine hypocrisy and double-standards because they have sanctioned the most vicious oppression in Ireland, supported dreadful carnage in Palestine committed by the State of Israel, and endorsed regime change in the Middle East that has unleashed a huge wave of sickening violence. There is another interpretive point to be reiterated here — unless they are pacifists, everyone accepts the utility of violence in certain circumstances. Of course, the conventional liberal mantra that "violence never solves anything" would not survive a moment's serious reflection and is only ever selectively applied by its protagonists, and it never seems to apply to those wielding the coercive power of the State. In terms of recent history, it has often been "liberals" who have cynically used violence on a massive scale, whilst perpetrating illegal wars and neo-imperialist expeditions. It is an uncomfortable fact that in recent years both Tony Blair and George Bush, the wretched former leaders of the "free, democratic West", have precipitated and inflicted far more murder, mayhem and misery than the hideous theological-fascist fundamentalists fighting for Al Qaeda or Islamic State. Anyone who fails to recognise this reality either has not been paying sufficient attention or is suffering from a deep-seated ethical self-delusion.

Whilst on the subject of violence, it might also be added that the current economic system has encoded within it a violence that actually destroys lives, and here the notion of "social murder" articulated by Friedrich Engels has a clear contemporary resonance. The market mechanism, as facilitated by a neoliberal State, involves relationships of power and coercion which ultimately inflicts great pain and suffering on people every single day. For example, the era of "austerity", as the government imposes stringent cuts in order to make ordinary people pay for the financial crisis caused by the banks, has led to lives being irreparably damaged and cut short. Indeed, austerity is, in effect, "a cruel and violent strategy of class domination" where "the life-shattering violence is caused by decisions that are made in Parliamentary chambers and government offices", and these devastating policies are "delivered by smartly dressed people sitting behind desks"[140]. Benefit sanctions, work capability assessments, foodbanks, homelessness and so on, are the consequence of the most appalling structural (slow, less visible) violence inflicted on the poor and vulnerable by an economic system that creates a vortex of "wants" without being able to meet the most basic of human needs. Where is the liberal outrage at this mundane, legitimised, structural violence inflicted upon society by the economic and political system? Their silence is deafening. So those of us who aspire to becoming part of a relevant (rather than liberal) left need not be squeamish about confronting the issue of direct physical (inter-personal) resistance — indeed, the failure to deploy all necessary measures to confront fascism effectively may consign us all to irrelevance.

The broader context:
Neoliberalism and the role of the State

The dominant liberal orthodoxy, which assumed that pluralistic, multicultural capitalism had ensured the permanent defeat of fascism, now looks exceedingly threadbare in the context of fascist and right-wing populist successes right across Europe, the USA and Latin America. There is evidence of a new populist zeitgeist emerging across the globe, reflected in the ascendancy of leaders like Trump, Orban and Bolsanaro. In effect the legacy of fascism is now being woven into the fabric of contemporary politics.

Such an observation means that it is important to address explicitly and reject the "failure of fascism" thesis which asserts that fascism was comprehensively and permanently defeated in 1945. For example, many academics and commentators subscribed to the comforting illusion that Britain's political culture is somehow immune to "extremism" and that "common sense" politics will always prevail. Indeed, the doyen of "fascist studies" Roger Griffin has argued that British people are far too sensible to be seduced by utopian and extremist ideologies and that the political culture militates against the assimilation of radical ideologies. In fact Griffin argued that the contextual conditions for fascism had effectively "disappeared for good"[141].

In many ways the "failure of fascism" hypothesis reflects the uncritical assimilation of a convenient cultural myth, or noble lie. The notion of fascist failure tends to obscure the fact that fascism has made some significant progress, has set the political agenda in some areas and retains the capacity to do serious damage to the social fabric. Indeed in terms of social attitudes, recent surveys have clearly indicated that the British public, amidst the chaos of Brexit, is "poised to embrace authoritarianism" and "right wing populism"[142]. Moreover, given the fact that it is the conservative elites, the people with power and privilege, who are most likely to succumb to the fatal allure of fascism during a period of crisis, the real concern is that the State itself may be controlled by social elements that are far more easily seduced by solutions that have much more in common with fascism than liberal democracy.

In this context it is important to note that the real threat of a more severely authoritarian future may not come directly from the neo-fascist micro-groups, although they retain a clear capacity to damage society, the genuine danger may come from a creeping coercive State which erodes human rights, and which moves the body politic towards the ideological territory inhabited by the far right. When this occurs, it makes it much easier for the noxious ideas of fascist micro-groups to gain traction. The State may be a complex (and sometimes contradictory) collection of institutions, organisations, processes and interactions (both repressive and ideological) but it is still possible to discern an overall strategic drift or direction of travel — an ostensibly liberal democratic State, which is unable to secure hegemony during a period of socio-economic and political crisis, may attempt to resolve this dilemma by moving toward a much more authoritarian, "exceptional" dispensation. Hence we need to acknowledge the potential of this dynamic to exert far more drastic and despotic State power.

We can in fact discern this process occurring now in the UK. The growth of officially sanctioned Islamophobia via counter-terrorism strategy, the expansion of the security agenda and the systematic erosion of civil liberties as a consequence of the so-called "war on terror" (which has necessitated the militarisation of the police, mass surveillance, secret courts, suspension of habeas corpus, extraordinary rendition, "black site" prisons, the use and justification of torture and extra-judicial assassination) all indicate unambiguously that the scope for a much more authoritarian version of liberal democracy is growing exponentially. Take as evidence the extent of the ethical dissembling that has occurred around the issue of torture and whether it might be legitimately deployed in response to threats to security. Such discussions would have been utterly unthinkable not so very long ago. It is not just that some people have been seduced into abandoning their moral sensibilities or are sleep-walking toward a condition of moral turpitude — the State itself as an instrument of repression and surveillance has effectively enhanced its own capabilities. All of this is, of course, underpinned by the sclerotic influence of secret State agencies which, having honed their craft during the years of colonial subjugation and Cold War, exist in a realm beyond the law where they remain largely unaccountable for their actions. This is why it is absolutely pointless to rely on State agencies and the law to deal with fascism whilst the State itself is moving in a proto-fascist direction.

As a result of the process outlined above the official ban imposed on National Action by the British government (which was wildly applauded by many liberals on "the left") will not work effectively, indeed it may actually be counter-productive in terms of preventing fascism. The very same fascists, who have been forced to abandon NA, will simply re-engage in other (new) groups and organisations which will, in essence, constitute NA in another, slightly modified guise[143]. Such a measure simply reflects the power of a State which has dramatically (and seemingly inexorably) enhanced its discretionary authority and coercive capacity to dictate the content of political discourse. It is interesting to note, for instance, that the UK's Prevent strategy outlines a list of "British values" which must be adhered to whilst in the USA the department of Homeland Security has already formally classified Antifa protests as "domestic terrorist violence". With the State effectively intervening to decide what are "appropriate" values and what is a legitimate political perspective, we seem to be heading into an area of jurisprudence previously examined by the infamous Nazi apologist Carl Schmitt. Schmitt outlined a so-called "friend-enemy thesis" whereby the State had the right and the power not only to identify threats to the State, but to suspend normal democratic procedures and protocols during a period of crisis. The logic of this presages the emergence of the "exceptional State" which formally dispenses with liberal pluralistic constraints upon central executive authority.

National Action may have articulated a genuinely nasty Nazi ideology, but it was largely ineffective, and the idea that State legislation is the best way to deal with the threat is an error. Proscribing the organisation is an entirely disproportionate response and feeds into a narrative which effectively endorses the expansion of a punitive, carceral State. The fact that governments have managed to secure widespread consent for an expansion in the coercive capacity of a State that works primarily on behalf of the wealthy and powerful is an instructive example of how hegemony is actually constructed, and the consequences are likely to be deleterious. By allowing the State to, in effect, determine the realm of "responsible" political discourse the State is able to effectively endorse the security agenda of those populist elements on right of the political spectrum, which will in turn make it much easier for genuine fascist (and even Nazi) ideas to gain leverage. In short, an official State ban, aiming to prevent a "vile ideology" in the name of liberal tolerance, may produce (in the longer term) precisely the opposite effect. In this way class power remains conveniently obscured by an ideologically manufactured consensus and then becomes disseminated throughout the entire fabric of social life — thereafter it is viewed as entirely normal, natural and beyond political contestation. It is not that such ideas are more persuasive, but that such "normality" often diminishes the capacity of people to make a rational choice because decisions have already been limited, and it becomes almost impossible to think beyond the system as it stands. In this way the State, in legitimating itself via perceptual distortion, can dominate society and effectively (attempt to) administer uncomfortable class contradictions out of existence. True insights into the political and economic structures are thereby thwarted or distorted and people are, in effect, reconciled to their subordinate location within the social system. The State "knows best" simply because no alternatives can be imagined. One of the consequences of this process is that the State has been given the primary role of dealing with the problem of fascism in society — in effect, we ended up giving a pyromaniac sole responsibility for putting fires out.

At this point it is crucial to acknowledge that the ballot box, or the size of fascist organisations are not the only matrix by which we might measure the success of fascist ideology. It is not that the liberal dams will be breached by a tidal wave of fascist votes, but that democratic values, institutions and processes are effectively eroded from within, thereby creating the conditions for fascist success in the future. The elliptical slide into a qualitatively different type of regime may be gradual and incremental, and in this sense the fascist lunatics on the fringes of the political spectrum do not need to do very much because the practical policy output of the State, which reflects and sustains asymmetrical power relationships, is moving the ideological centre of gravity in their direction.

The contemporary liberal democratic State in Britain, whilst deploying the rhetoric of "security, safety and stability" is moving toward an altogether more sinister proto-fascist formulation. Moreover, right-wing discontent at failure to deliver an adequate Brexit might be the final catalyst that alters, in a qualitative sense, the configuration of the State. It is always worth remembering that ultimately the State's polycontextual function, despite its existence as a site of political struggle reflecting wider social contradictions, is to protect the material interests of the dominant class — to ensure, more specifically, social stability and the economic conditions conducive to continued capital accumulation. It is also a fact that in global terms, where free market capitalism is dominant, the authoritarian conception of the State is far more prevalent than the liberal democratic model. Capitalism's connection to democratic forms and structures is (and has always been) tenuous and contingent upon a range of factors which are difficult to predict or control. So there is no impenetrable wall of liberal tolerance separating conventional politics from fascism in Britain, despite the comforting assurances of some politicians, journalists and academics. Certainly, the neoliberal political project which emphasises austerity and security has precipitated a dynamic which is driving democracy toward a more dictatorial form which attempts to (re)exert control by ossifying the balance of social forces in favour of capital. If the State fails in its primary function to maintain social relations favourable to the accumulation of capital, and if the democratic process is incapable of securing this outcome, then there are always alternative, more authoritarian, options.

The reality is that unrestrained capitalism makes it much more difficult to solve the problem of violent right-wing micro-groups because the economic system, which produces dramatic levels of social inequality, and which is systemically prone to intermittent cyclical crises, actually incubates the fascist contagion. Neoliberalism as the dominant economic orthodoxy has heralded a new age of social asymmetry where a few dozen super-rich billionaires, with trillions hidden away in assorted off-shore tax-havens, own more wealth than half the world's population. Capitalist society is entirely configured for the benefit of these parasites. While the rich convince themselves that a meritocracy has rewarded their own perspicacity and endeavour, the poor internalise their status as failed consumers. Here the ignorant, narcissistic vulgarity of Trump, as "leader of the free world" is the perfect symbol of a putrid "liberal" democracy and the selfish hyper-individuality which provides the dynamic for Western capitalism. In the capitalist market place, where private interaction is seen as the only legitimate and viable means of human agency and the only way of organising economic activity, labour is commodified in a profit-loss calculus, and everything is effectively submerged in the icy water of egoistic calculation. Where capitalism prevails, the free market has the status of a revealed truth or a force of nature, like gravity or the weather. However, this interaction of "free" individuals has led, not to abundant economic benefits available to all, as envisaged by the likes of Friedrich Hayek, but to a dystopian nightmare where life for most people is likely to be "solitary, poor, nasty, brutish and short". This is actually the real "road to serfdom". The idea that the market is an impartial omniscient algorithm able to produce the best of all possible worlds has always been a convenient fiction, and the truth is that unfettered markets result in the obscene moral travesty of hedge fund managers receiving billions while nurses rely on foodbanks. Capitalism, to paraphrase Oscar Wilde, knows the price of everything and the value of nothing.

In such an economic context there is an inevitable populist impulse to blame immigrants and refugees for resource scarcity. Ubiquitous cynicism about conventional Parliamentary politics and the febrile atmosphere precipitated by Brexit has meant the scope for "radical" alternatives has expanded exponentially. In this situation, the fascist far right offers seductively simplistic solutions to complex socio-economic problems. However, there is a much broader socio-political observation to be made in the context of increasing far right political activity. In order to effectively eliminate the threat posed by the disciples of new wave Nazi ideology, the contemporary political consensus on how society is organised and the utility of free market capitalism requires substantive re-evaluation

— neoliberalism as an ideology needs to be confronted and comprehensively defeated, and the "vampire capitalist" system which creates shocking inequality whilst precipitating global ecological disaster, needs to be destroyed and replaced with a far more rational method of distributing resources[144].

In conclusion, activists who focus entirely on the stubborn persistence of the pathological misfits and morons who inhabit the Nazi micro-groups, whilst ignoring the nature of the State and the socio-economic and political context within which such activity takes place, not only diminish our chance of understanding why these groups emerge, it effectively exonerates those who have been complicit in creating an environment within which such ideas and groups can flourish. There is an entirely understandable urge to recoil at the message conveyed by groups like National Action, but they are unlikely to disappear completely unless the socio-political and economic environment which keeps producing such micro-groups is adequately addressed. Such an approach is an essential component for the accurate cognition which is a prerequisite for the successful emancipation from such forces. Max Horkheimer once famously remarked that anyone who won't talk about capitalism should stay quiet about fascism — the corollary of that is, of course, that if you want to talk genuine anti-fascism, you have to talk anti-capitalism. Recognising the importance of exogenous factors when examining the ideology of particular political groups is a prerequisite for any deeper understanding of their purpose and prospects, and this needs to be emphasised if explanations are to acquire appropriate depth, complexity and clarity. Indeed, disregarding the deeper contextual dimensions of fascist activity is not only an impediment to effective analysis, it is a pusillanimous dereliction of duty. Of course, anti-fascists need to focus their strategy on the fascist organisations themselves, but also on the State/society which provides the context within which this conflict is being played out. In the age of austerity, where the attempt to re-impose neoliberalism after the financial crisis has exposed the naked class interests which underpin the capitalist economic system, nothing is more important than understanding the nature of the threat from the far right. We need to deal effectively with fascists, and this means replacing, once and for all, the predatory economic system that causes such misery and periodically vomits forth this vile ideology.

NO PASARAN!

~ **M J Hayes**

Proscription and its outcomes

In the following supplementary text 12 Rules For What? *outlines the direct results of the proscription of National Action, looking at what happened to the remnants of the group and impacts on neo-Nazi tactics over the last few years.*

The proscription of an organisation under the Terrorism Act 2000 is one of the most authoritarian legal instruments available to the British State. The decision to proscribe a group is at the discretion of the Home Secretary, who has to take into account factors such as the nature and scale of the group, the threat it poses to the country and the threat to British nationals overseas, to justify the order. Once a group is proscribed, it immediately becomes illegal either to be a member or support the group, wear clothing or displaying items which could arouse suspicion that you are a member of a proscribed group, or give it moral support or approval. Penalties for these offences are severe. Membership or support of a proscribed group attracts a prison sentence of up to ten years and an unlimited fine. Wearing an article of clothing that even suggests membership lands a prison sentence of up to six months and a fine of up to £5,000.

Proscription is not particularly uncommon. There are 71 organisations currently proscribed by the UK, and the government usually bans groups to little fanfare. National

Action, however, is notable for being the first far-right group banned since the Second World War, leaving out the various loyalist terror groups banned under separate legislation. Their proscription also signalled an increased interest on the part of the British State in far-right extremist activity. Referrals of the far-right to the Home Office's counter-extremism programme, Prevent, have risen in the last three years from 10 to 18% of the total. In September 2019, Britain's lead counter-terrorism police officer declared far-right extremism the fastest growing threat in the UK. And in 2018 MI5, the domestic security service, took over responsibility for investigating far-right terror activity from counter-terrorism police, a change which means far-right terrorism is now treated as the same level threat to national security as Islamist and North of Ireland terror activity. The involvement of MI5 means far-right extremists face a new force, one with greater powers to surveil and investigate and a level of institutional expertise grounded in decades of work in the North of Ireland and against Islamist groups.

The aftermath of proscription

Proscription in December 2016 heralded a wave of State repression against National Action and its leadership and signalled increased interest in far-right extremism on the part of the government's counter-extremism agencies. Throughout 2017 and 2018, the British State carried out a series of arrests and investigations of activists associated with the group. In 2018, ten people, including the leader Christopher Lythgoe, were convicted of membership of the organisation and received sentences of four to eight years in prison. These trials received widespread media attention due to National Action's notoriety and the extreme racism of those on trial. Most outlandish of all were the couple Claudia Patatas and Adam Thomas, who named their newborn child Adolf and took photos with Nazi flags and KKK robes.

A conviction that received particular attention was that of Corporal Mikko Vehvilainen, a serving member of the armed forces who acted as a recruiter for National Action and was discovered with a photo of himself giving a Nazi salute and swastika bunting in his house. He was also hoarding a cache of weapons. While liberal hand wringing over reactionary influence on the British Army is laughable, the army not being a particularly progressive institution, it is still notable that National Action had identified a natural base so close to the State from which to recruit.

The case of Jack Renshaw is perhaps the most widely known. Renshaw started his political career in the youth wing of the British National Party, then an increasingly irrelevant force on the far right after their collapse in the polls in 2010. He switched allegiance to National Action in 2016, following ex-BNP Youth activist and National Action founder Alex Davies, and quickly became a public spokesperson for the group. Renshaw had already expressed antisemitic views in blog posts in 2014 and continued his extremist rhetoric in speeches on public demonstrations. While investigating

Renshaw after his initial arrest in January 2017 the police discovered evidence that he had been grooming teenage boys for sex and interviewed him again in May 2017.

By July 2017, with the investigations into child grooming and racial hatred closing in, Renshaw had devised a plot to murder the Labour MP Rosie Cooper and a woman police officer who was involved in the investigations against him. He had bought a 19-inch knife and had recorded a message to be released after his death — he planned to "suicide by cop" wearing a fake suicide vest — dying as a martyr to the Nazi cause. However, when Renshaw revealed his plans to fellow National Action members at Wetherspoons one attendee, Robbie Mullen, reported the plan to the anti-racist charity Hope Not Hate, who passed the information on to the police. In January 2018 Renshaw received a sentence of three years for two counts of inciting racial hatred. In May 2019, Renshaw was sentenced to life imprisonment with a minimum term of 20 years for preparing and act of terrorism and threatening to kill a police officer. After the sentencing it emerged that in June 2018 he had been convicted of four counts of inciting a child to engage in sexual activity for which he received an 18 month sentence.

New groupings

Before National Action was proscribed, the journalist James Poulter predicted in an article for Vice that a state ban would "unleash a wave of repression that the far-right has never experienced before in the UK." His prediction has been borne out. Key figures in National Action will be in prison for significant lengths of time and there is no denying that National Action's activism has been significantly curtailed.

However, would-be far-right terrorists have not disappeared with the proscription. Later in his article Poulter further predicted that "it's likely an autonomous neo-Nazi network will emerge, which will include members of both these groups and potentially a number of people currently on their fringes. If groups like this get outlawed, that doesn't mean they go away". Although National Action is no longer functioning, key figures in the group escaped any kind of legal blowback from their activities and continued to organise. National Action was able to use the proscription as a demonstration of their dangerousness to the society they opposed (one of the primary markers of legitimacy for groups on the extreme right). Since the proscription of National Action in December 2016 the threat of far-right terrorism has not gone away.

In March 2017, an undercover investigation by ITV News discovered that activists associated with National Action were still meeting in secret, and had organised a training weekend for themselves and their supporters. Not long after National Action was outlawed, two other groups — Scottish Dawn and NS131 (National Socialist Anti-Capitalist Action) — were established and operated until they were also proscribed as aliases of National Action in September 2017. This tactic of changing one's name is copied directly from the previous target of proscription orders — Islamic terrorist groups.

In June 2019, two members of Sonnenkreig Division, another post-National Action group inspired by the American neo-Nazi group Attomwaffen Division, were convicted of terror offences for praising Anders Brevik and encouraging attacks against Jewish people and people of colour. In September 2019, another group, Feuerkrieg Division, circulated a list of police buildings on the encrypted messaging service Telegram and called for reprisal attacks in retaliation for the arrest of a 16-year-old Nazi. The group, having retained National Action's penchant for outrageous imagery, also sent a picture of the Chief Constable of West Midlands police with a gun to his head and the words "race traitor" emblazoned across his eyes.

New conditions for the far right

By taking away the ability to openly organise, the state limited the options of the members of National Action, who are then likely to turn to even more extreme activities. Arguably, the suppression of public-facing activities has exacerbated a turn in the far right towards terrorism. The atomisation effect that proscription has on groups pushes them towards increasingly difficult-to-stop violence. There is already a relatively low barrier to committing mass violence if an individual or group has the will, and security services are not infallible. However, it is easier to thwart a group intent on committing a terror attack than an individual — as shown by attacks in Norway, Christchurch, and Pittsburgh, and by the murder of Jo Cox MP in 2016. This turn to terrorism arguably puts far-right groups beyond the reaches of traditional antifascist tactics.

It was National Action's response to the death of Cox that was the direct cause of their proscription, Tweeting "Only 649 MPs to go #WhiteJihad" and changing their listing on Google search results to the slogan Cox's killer uttered at a court hearing: "Death to traitors, freedom for Britain." This is part of a wider trend in their propaganda, towards ever more pointed and direct claims to violence. It was their very public-facing propagandistic activity that lead to them being proscribed as opposed to other groups more directly connected with Cox's killer.

It is likely that their proscription was not the only cause of their move into smaller and smaller groupings. Indeed, before proscription, National Action had already pivoted away from public organising. National Action wasn't interested in growing, it was interested in intensifying — driving its members and supporters to an extremity of ideology and action. There is an important distinction between groups whose main intention is to commit extreme actions and groups that want to find a broad public base for their politics. An order that is targeted mostly at public activities and rhetoric will have little effect on an organisation uninterested in growth — and indeed will likely drive the organisation towards radicalisation.

Before the internet, extreme far-right organisations had limited means to spread their message. Paper sales, public meetings and demonstrations could be easily monitored, and are susceptible to disruption by state agencies, as well as by well-organised opposition. In a time of encrypted messaging services, anonymous message boards, and offshore domain hosting, blunt instruments like proscription have become less effective as far right activists have turned to secure means of organising that are harder for the State to monitor and disrupt.

Conclusion — Anti-fascist research

Proscription makes it harder for anti-fascists to oppose the far right. While anti-fascists across the UK were successful in opposing National Action's marches and stunts before proscription, the turn towards underground organising is more difficult. There are no immediate answers to the question of what an anti-fascist response outside of the state can do.

However, parts of the path forward are clear. Anti-fascists need to develop new competencies in research and monitoring. We believe it is an essential part of any anti-fascist movement that it be able to precisely and thoroughly know its enemy. This means both research at a high level — acquiring information about groups and their activities — and at a low level — understanding the particular individuals who make the groups up. It also includes understanding the disputes and conflicts within and between groups, which are often the source of considerable tension on the far right.

In the US, there is a much more substantial culture of research, monitoring, and doxxing (publishing the names of far-right activists) by anti-fascists of the far right. These tactics have been effective at blunting a surge in far-right activity there, exposing members of the far right to both social shaming, the loss of jobs, and other reprisals. After the Unite the Right rally in Charlottesville, there was a wave of doxxing of far right activists. It was almost certainly in part this that made the attempted repetition of the event the following year such an extraordinary embarrassment for the far right.

A model for action can be found in Redox, a Danish anti-fascist research group that places itself within the militant antifascist movement. As a research collective, Redox provides information on fascist groups to any progressive organisation, network or initiative and has an expressed purpose to strengthen the left's opposition to the far right. In many respects Redox is a professional news gathering organisation that is funded by private donations, progressive unions, fundraisers and sales of publications. With solid funding, Redox has been effective in being able to dedicate time and resources to the project, whilst still being embedded within militant antifascism.

How can anti-fascists in the UK do similarly? Already, there are signs of increased awareness of the problem. Autonomous anti-fascists have been pooling information, but there is an urgent need for widespread collaboration and an organised national antifascist research group to carry this work forward. This is not a complete solution to the problem of far-right extremism. Research does not convert straightforwardly into disruption, nor does research uncover everything. Given the substantially greater resources of the state to do such work, and their failure rate, this is evident. But it is an essential step towards building a robust and complete anti-fascist movement, with a diversity of responses to the diversity of far-right groups it must oppose.

REFERENCES

1] see B. Quinn, J. Grierson, D. Gayle (2019) "Far right terrorists are one step ahead of you in UK, police told" *Guardian* April 5th theguardian.com

2] Matthew Collins, in his recent book, describes NA as "deadly serious about terrorism" and states unequivocally that "death and terror had become their only obsessions". See M. Collins (2019) *Nazi Terrorist: The Story of National Action* Hope Not Hate. See P. Jackson (2014-15) "#hitlerwasright: National Action and National Socialism for the 21st Century" *Journal for Deradicalisation* Winter No.1 p.98

3] Home Office (2016) Proscribed Terrorist Organisations London Home Office. A six month sentence or a fine of £5,000 can be imposed for wearing clothing, carrying symbols or displaying articles which indicate support for any proscribed group. V.Dodd (2018) "MI5 to take over in fight against rise of UK right-wing extremists" *Guardian* 28 October theguardian.com. See D. Gadher (2016) "Warning over rise of Hitler youth" *Sunday Times* 20 November, C. England (2016) "British neo-Nazi group National Action banned by Home Secretary under terror laws" *Independent* 12 December. Rudd, deploying the rhetoric of "security" and "risk", said that NA "promotes a vile ideology and I will not stand for it", see Elgot, J. (2016) "National Action banned by UK Home Secretary" *Guardian* Monday 12 December. Two "aliases" for the group, Scottish Dawn and NS131, were also banned in September 2017 (see *BBC News* 28 Sept 2017 "Two neo-Nazi groups added to banned list" bbc.co.uk; see also L. Dearden "Banned neo-Nazi terrorist groups still recruiting as aliases of National Action" *Independent* 29 September 2017). Other aliases have included System Resistance Network (SRN) and Vanguard Britannia. See also C. Allen (2018) "Proscribing National Action: has it been effective?" *Open Democracy UK* 19 October opendemocracy.net, S. Hopkins (2017) "National Action: How Neo-Nazi Group went from an open joke to an Alleged Army-Trained Terror Threat" *Huffington* Post huffingtonpost.co.uk. Grierson (2018) outlines that "Prevent referrals over right-wing extremism rise by over a third" *Guardian* 13 December theguardian.com; and see also D. Gayle (2018) "UK fascists modelled on jihadis are prepared to kill, say campaigners" *Guardian* 2 February the guardian.com, who quotes the government's Joint Terrorism Analysis Centre.

4] see N. Copsey (2008) *Contemporary British Fascism: The British National Party and the Quest for Legitimacy* Basingstoke, Palgrave Macmillan; M. Goodwin (2011) *New British Fascism: Rise of the British National Party* London, Routledge; M. Goodwin (2010) "In search of the winning formula: Nick Griffin and the 'modernisation' of the British National Party" in R. Eatwell and M. Goodwin (eds) *The New Extremism in Twenty-First Century* Britain Abingdon, Routledge Chapter 8 pp.169-90; D. Trilling (2012) *Bloody Nasty People: The Rise of Britain's Far Right* London, Verso; R. Eatwell (2004) "The extreme right in Britain: The long road to 'modernisation'" in R. Eatwell and C. Mudde (eds) *Western Democracies and the New Extreme Right Challenge* London, Routledge Chapter 3 pp.62-79; M. Hayes (2014) *The Ideology of Fascism and the Far Right in Britain* Ottawa, Red Quill Books. See also A. Mammone (2009) "The Eternal Return? Faux Populism and Contemporarization of Neo-Fascism across Britain, France and Italy" *Journal of Contemporary European Studies* 17/2 pp.171-92

5] P. Jackson (2014) "Accumulative Extremism: The Post-War Tradition of Anglo-American Neo-Nazi Activism" Chapter 1 in P. Jackson and A. Shekhovtsov (eds) *The Postwar Anglo-American Far Right* Basingstoke, Palgrave Macmillan p.3

6] C. Cortbus (2014) "Nazis Now on Campus" *The Huffington Post* 29 April huffpost.com. See S. Wright, B. Glaze and C. Cortbus (2014) "Exposed: Rise of Hitler-loving National Action group who want to 'ethnically cleanse' the UK" *Daily Mirror* 7 June mirror.co.uk

7] M. Collins (2015) "National Action: Young, Nazi and Dangerous" *HOPE not hate* March/April hopenothate.org.uk. See P. Jackson (2014-15) op cit pp.97-115

8] NA national-action.info nd "Attack" p. 3 and p.16

9] Benjamin Raymond cited in Collins (2015) op cit

10] Collins (2015) op cit

11] NA national-action.info "What is National Action?" *Joint Statement* 2016

12] Raymond cited in NA national-action.info 2015

13] *see* NA national-action.info *Monthly Archive* January 2014, and Raymond cited in NA national-action.info 2015

14] NA national-action.info *Joint Statement* 2016

15] NA national-action.info "Strategy and Promotion" 2013

16] NA national-action.info nd "Attack" p.22

17] ibid p.39

18] *Radio Aryan*/dailystormer.com 2016 Alex Davies (interview) 2 February. There is evidence NA had a useful source of funding via the North West Infidels' connection to the local drug trade. See Collins (2019) op cit.

19] see NA national-action.info Monthly Archive January 2014

20] Radio Aryan 2016 op cit

21] NA national-action.info Yearly Review 2014

22] ibid

23] Jackson (2014-15) op cit p.106

24] NA national-action.info "Strategy and Promotion" 2013

25] See E. Turner-Graham (2015) "Subcultural style: Fashion and Britain's extreme right" Chapter 7 in N. Copsey and J. Richardson (eds) (2015) *Cultures of Post-War British Fascism* Abingdon, Routledge p.129

26] NA national-action.info "Strategy and Promotion" 2013, see D. Gadher, J. Boswell and J. Lyons (2016) "Far right calls for white jihad" *Sunday Times* 26 June

27] cited in Hopkins (2017) op cit and ibid. See J. Lyons (2016) "Far right hijacks MP's murder for Brexit" *Sunday Times* 19 June

28] NA national-action.info nd "Attack" p.21

29] Raymond cited in Collins (2015) op cit

30] Raymond cited in NA national-action.info 2015

31] see NA national-action.info Yearly Review 2016. See NA national-action.info Yearly Review 2014

32] The Liverpool demonstration did not go according to plan and NA took refuge, under police protection, in the lost luggage collection point at Lime Street Station after being confronted by anti-fascists, see S. Hopkins (2015) "Liverpool: White Man March Neo-Nazis Cower in Station Depot After Being Pelted With Rubbish, Then Cancel Event" *The Huffington Post* 15 August huffpost.com; S. McCoid (2015) "Neo-Nazis threaten Liverpool race riots if Mayor Joe Anderson cancels city centre march" *Liverpool Echo* 9 August. As the NA website put it "... by a miracle we were all left unscathed. Other groups and contingents were not so lucky..." and "if anything our enemies failed to capitalise on a golden opportunity to crush us once and for all" NA national-action. info Monthly Archive August 2015

33] NA national-action.info Monthly Archive December 2013

34] see Cortbus (2014) op cit. In terms of "events" organised by NA , there is clearly some exaggeration for effect by both the (local) media and the group itself, but the fact that such activities took place is beyond reasonable doubt.

35] see *Radio Aryan* (2016) op cit

36] K. Connolly and P. Oltermann (2016) "British far right group posts photo of Nazi salute at Buchenwald" *Guardian* Thursday 26 May, see S. Hopkins (2016) "Nazi Salute at Buchenwald Death Camp could lead to National Action Members being jailed in Germany" *The Huffington Post* 26 May huffpost.com

37] see NA national-action.info "Strategy and Promotion" 2013

38] Fenek Solere cited in NA national-action.info Monthly Archive April 2016

39] see J. Kaplan (1997) "Leaderless Resistance" *Terrorism and Political Violence* autumn vol 9 No.3 pp.80-95. It is worth remembering that this tactic has been used before in a British context. David Copeland, who was linked to Combat 18, engaged in a nail bomb campaign in 2019.

40] NA national-action.info nd "Attack" p.23. NA activists have engaged in and planned a number of violent attacks. For example, in 2015 NA supporter Zack Davies was convicted of attempted murder in Flintshire. His victim was a Sikh man and Davies claimed it was "revenge" for the murder of Lee Rigby. The fact that the victim was not a Muslim did not appear to bother Davies because he "looked Asian". NA follower Garron Helm was also jailed in 2014 for sending abusive anti-Semitic messages and death threats to Luciana Berger, MP for Wavertree. Helm was subsequently disowned by NA (perhaps because he said in court he was "deeply remorseful"). See A. Rouse (2014) "'Unmasked': Merseysider jailed for anti-Semitic tweet to Luciana Berger shows 'dark side'" *Liverpool Echo* 20 October. In October 2017 several NA leaders, including serving members of the British army, were charged with being activists in the "terror group" and one, Christopher Lythgoe, was charged with encouragement to commit murder (see *BBC News* 5 September 2017 "Neo-Nazi arrests: National Action suspects are in the army", bbc.co.uk; also *Evening Standard* 27 October 2017). In April 2019 NA member Jack Renshaw, a convicted paedophile, was convicted of an attempt to murder Rosie Cooper MP see B. Quinn (2019) "Hope not Hate spy played a key role in stopping far right plot to murder MP" *Guardian* 3 April theguardian.com.

41] Collins (2015) op cit

42] NA national-action.info nd "Attack" p.12

43] ibid p.14

44] NA national-action.info Monthly Archive January 2014

45] Kai Murros cited in NA national-action.info Monthly Archive April 2016

46] Raymond cited in NA national-action.info 2015

47] NA national-action.info Yearly Review 2014

48] ibid

49] NA national-action.info nd "Attack" p.5

50] ibid p.14

51] NA Homepage (2014) cited in Jackson (2014-15) op cit p.111 and p.107

52] NA national-action.info Monthly Archive September 2013, NA national-action.info Yearly Review 2014

53] NA national-action.info Monthly Archive October 2013

54] NA "Attack" (2014) cited in Jackson (2014-15) op cit p.112

55] see NA national-action.info nd "Attack" p.7

56] see ibid

57] NA national-action.info Yearly Review 2014

58] NA national-action.info

59] NA national-action.info Monthly Archive January 2014

60] NA national-action.info nd "Attack" p.43

61] NA national-action.info Monthly Archive October 2013, NA national-action.info nd "Attack" p.7

62] NA national-action.info nd "Attack" p.17

63] see NA national-action.info Monthly Archive April 2016

64] NA national-action.info Monthly Archive October 2013

65] see NA national-action.info Joint Statement 2016

66] NA national-action.info Monthly Archive September 2013

67] see ibid August 2013

68] see ibid August 2015. NA ran a female "beauty" competition entitled "Miss Hitler".

69] see ibid January 2014

70] see Jackson (2014-15) op cit p.110

71] see NA national-action.info "Strategy and Promotion" 2013

72] NA national-action.info Monthly Archive December 2015

73] ibid September 2013

74] ibid

75] Raymond cited in NA national-action.info 2015

76] NA national-action.info Yearly Review 2014

77] NA national-action.info *Joint Statement* 2016

78] cited in NA national-action.info Monthly Archive April 2016

79] Fenek Solere in ibid December 2015

80] ibid November 2015

81] NA national-action.info Monthly Archive April 2016

82] ibid September 2013

83] see ibid November 2015

84] ibid December 2015

85] ibid April 2016

86] ibid September 2013

87] ibid April 2016

88] Fenek Solere in ibid November 2015

89] ibid

90] ibid

91] NA national-action.info Monthly Archive September 2013

92] see NA national-action.info 2015

93] NA national-action.info nd "Attack" p.41

94] NA national-action.info Yearly Review 2014

95] Jackson 2014-15 op cit p.104

96] NA national-action.info Monthly Archive January 2014

97] NA "Nationalism is for Stormtroopers" cited in L. Sherriff (2014) "Meet the New Neo-Nazi Group National Action Which Just Wants to 'Piss People Off'" *The Huffington Post* 6 March huffpost.com

98] see Jackson (2014-15) op cit p.104

99] see NA national-action.info Monthly Archive November 2015

100] see ibid

101] see ibid

102] ibid April 2016

103] see ibid May 2016

104] NA national-action.info Yearly Review 2014

105] see NA national-action.info nd "Attack" p.8

106] NA national-action.info Monthly Archive April 2016. See ibid November 2015

107] NA national-action.info "Strategy and Promotion" 2013

108] ibid, NA national-action.info Yearly Review 2014

109] Friedrich Holderin cited in NA national-action.info Monthly Archive April 2016

110] NA national-action.info Monthly Archive September 2013

111] ibid December 2015

112] ibid July 2015

113] NA national-action.info "Strategy and Promotion" 2013

114] See A. Hitler (1961) *Hitler's Secret Book* New York, Grove Press, A. Hitler (1961) *The Testament of Adolf Hitler: The Hitler-Bormann Documents* London, Cassell; A. Hitler (1973) *Table Talk 1941-1944*

London, Weidenfeld and Nicolson; A. Hitler (1974) *Mein Kampf* London, Hutchinson. See also N. H. Baynes (1969) *The Speeches of Adolf Hitler* Volumes I and II New York, H.Fertig

115] The BUF was formed in 1932 by Oswald Mosley and represented the most developed and serious example of fascism in Britain. The organisation, which aimed to emulate the success of Mussolini and Hitler, precipitated widespread opposition (e.g. Cable Street 1936). It was proscribed by the government under Defence Regulation 18B in 1940. The NF, formed in 1967, briefly became the fourth largest political party in the 1970s but saw significant ideological and factional splits in the 1980s. The BNP was founded in 1982 and had significant electoral success in the 2000s with its populist ethno-nationalist ideology. Internal controversy over financial irregularity saw its support base decline dramatically after 2010. See Hayes (2014) op cit, see also R. Griffin (1996) "British Fascism: The Ugly Duckling" in M. Cronin (ed) (1996) *The Failure of British Fascism: The Far Right and the Fight for Political Recognition* Basingstoke, Palgrave Macmillan Chapter 8 pp.141-65; R. Griffin (2000) "Interregnum or Endgame? Radical Right Thought in the 'Post-Fascist' Era" *Journal of Political Ideologies* July vol 5 No.2 pp.163-78; R. Griffin (2002) "The Incredible Shrinking Ism: The Survival of Fascism in the Post-Fascist Era" *Patterns of Prejudice* vol 36 No.3 pp.3-8

116] See O. Mosley (1934) *The Greater Britain* London, BUF/Jeffcoats; O. Mosley (1938) *Tomorrow We Live* London, Black House Publishing; O. Mosley (1946) *My Answer* Ramsbury, Mosley Publications; O. Mosley (1947) *The Alternative* Ramsbury, Mosley Publications

117] see D. Holland (1984) *The Political Soldier* NF Nat Ed Group. See Hepple, T. (1989) *From Ballots to Bombs: The Inside Story of the National Front's Political Soldiers* London, Searchlight Publishing; D. Baker (1985) "A.K. Chesterton, The Strasser Brothers, and the Politics of the National Front" *Patterns of Prejudice* 19 No.3 pp.3-12

118] see R. Eatwell (1996) "The Esoteric Ideology of the National Front in the 1980s" in M. Cronin (ed) *The Failure of British Fascism* London, Palgrave Macmillan Chapter 6 pp.99-117; see also O. Strasser (1940) *Hitler and I* London, Cape; O. Strasser (1940) *Germany Tomorrow* London, Cape. The Terza Posizione ("Third Position") was designed to denote an ideological perspective that was neither capitalist nor communist (sometimes referred to as "National Bolshevism").

119] The name Combat 18 was derived from the first and eighth letters of the alphabet "A" and "H" — Adolf Hitler.

120] internal C18 documentation, seen by the author, focused on the reasons for their failure to defeat the forces ranged against them, described Red Action, a key component of AFA, as "drunken Red Fenians". As an ex-member I can confirm this assertion is only partially accurate because we were never drunk! See M. Hayes (2014) "Red Action — left wing pariah: some observations regarding ideological apostasy and the discourse of proletarian resistance" Chapter 12 in E. Smith and M. Worley (eds) *Against the Grain: The British far left from 1956* Manchester, Manchester University Press

121] NA national-action.info Monthly Archive December 2015; see T. Linehan (2012) "Space Matters: Spatialising British Fascism" *Socialist History* 41 pp.1-21

122] NA national-action.info Monthly Archive March 2016

123] Anti-Fascist Action was the most prominent and effective of those groups opposing fascism both physically and ideologically. This success was due to the nature of its engagement with working class communities, organisational preparation and tactical precision. See S. Birchall (2010) *Beating the Fascists: The Untold Story of Anti-Fascist Action* London, Freedom Press. See also M. Hayes and P. Aylward (2000) "Anti-Fascist Action: Radical Resistance or Rent-a-Mob?" *Soundings* Issue 14 Spring pp.53-62; N. Lowles (2001) *White Riot: The Violent History of Combat 18* Bury, Milo Books; K. Bullstreet (2001) *Bash the Fash: Anti-Fascist Recollections 1984-93* London, Kate Sharpley Library. The success of anti-fascist strategy has been the subject of some academic debate: see N. Copsey (2000) *Anti-Fascism in Britain* Basingstoke, Macmillan; N. Copsey (2011) "From Direct Action to Community Action: The changing dynamics of anti-fascist opposition" in N. Copsey and G. Macklin (eds) *British National Party: Contemporary Perspectives* London, Routledge Chapter 6 pp.123-41; R. Eatwell (2010) "Responses to the extreme right in Britain" in Eatwell and Goodwin (eds) op cit Chapter 10 pp.211-30. See Cronin (1996) op cit and Hayes (2014) op cit.

124] NA national-action.info Monthly Archive January 2014; NA cited in Cortbus (2014) op cit

125] see P. Gattinara, C. Froio and M. Albanese (2013) "The appeal of Neo-Fascism in times of crisis: The experience of CasaPound Italia" *Fascism* vol 2 issue 2 pp.234-58, see NA national-action.info Monthly Archive April 2016. See also J. Bale (2002) "National Revolutionary Groupuscules and the Resurgence of Left-Wing Fascism: The Case of France's Nouvelle Resistance" *Patterns of Prejudice* 36/3 pp.22-49

126] In this way connections were established and sustained with groups like Atomwaffen Division in the USA. See Jackson (2014) op cit p.30. *See* C. Atton (2006) "Far Right Media on the internet: cultures, discourse and power" *New Media and Society* vol 18 (4) pp.573-87

127] Jackson (2014-15) op cit p.101

128] ibid p.105-6

129] ibid p.113

130] ibid p.111, see Jackson (2014) op cit p.6. See R. Griffin (1999) "Fascism is more than reaction" *Searchlight* September pp.24-26, and R. Griffin (2000) "Revolution from the Right: Fascism" in D. Parker (ed) *Revolutions and the Revolutionary Tradition in the West 1560-1991* London, Routledge pp.185-201.

131] NA national-action.info Monthly Archive December 2015

132] NA national-action.info nd "Attack" p.7; NA national-action.info Monthly Archive September 2013

133] see Hayes (2014) op cit

134] Collins (2015) op cit; see M. Collins (2006) "When is a terrorist not a terrorist? When he is a Nazi" *Searchlight* September No.375 pp.8-9. See Hayes (2014) op cit, also N. Bobbio (1996) *Left and Right: The Significance of Political Distinction* Cambridge, Polity Press

135] Raymond cited in NA national-action.info 2015

136] see S. Nelson (2017) "Noam Chomsky: Antifa is a 'major gift to the right'" *Washington Examiner* August 17. See also M. Testa (2017) "'A Good Deal of Disorder' or The Anarchist and Anti-Fascism in the UK" *Anarchist Studies* 25 2 pp.9-25

137] S. Zizek (2017) "Today's anti-fascist movement will do nothing to get rid of right wing populism — it's just panicky posturing" Independent 7 December. See S. Zizek (2014) "Only a radicalised left can save Europe" *New Statesman* 25 June www.newstatesman.com

138] S. Zizek cited in T. Wofford (2017) "Philosopher Slavoj Zizek settles the 'Is it ok to punch a Nazi' question once and for all" *QZ&A* January qz.com

139] see Birchall (2010) op cit, see also N. Copsey (2018) "Militant Antifascism: An Alternative (Historical) Reading" *Society* 55 pp.243-47

140] V. Cooper and D. Whyte (2017) *The Violence of Austerity* Pluto p.27, p.1, p.23

141] cited in Hayes (2014) op cit p.416-17

142] P. Walker (2019) "UK poised to embrace authoritarianism, warns Hansard society" *Guardian* 8 April theguardian.com. See S. Tisdall (2019) "Populists are whipping up a storm as Europe faces lurch to the right" *Guardian* 6 April theguardian.com. The utter vacuity of the liberal left is conveniently illustrated by Tisdall with his pathetic request for people to endorse Macron as a more "tolerant" alternative to the "anger mongers" of the far right.

143] Groups such as Sonnenkreig. As NA leader Christopher Lythgoe said, regarding the impact of the official ban: "we're just shedding one skin for another", cited in Collins (2019) op cit. See L. Dearden (2019) "National Action: Factions of neo-Nazi terrorist group active more than two years after government ban" *Independent* 27 April

144] See P. Kennedy (2017) *Vampire Capitalism: Fractured Societies and Alternative Futures* London, Palgrave Macmillan; R. Evans (2019) "Half of England is owned by less than 1% of the population" *Guardian* 17 April theguardian.com